The Art and Science Connection

Hands-On Activities for Intermediate Students

Kimberley Tolley

Innovative Learning Publications

Addison-Wesley Publishing Company

Menlo Park, California • Reading, Massachusetts • New York
Don Mills, Ontario • Wokingham, England • Amsterdam • Bonn
Paris • Milan • Madrid • Sydney • Singapore • Tokyo
Seoul • Taipei • Mexico City • San Juan

This book is dedicated to Emma and Nathan, and to everyone who enjoys *both* art and science.

Acknowledgments

I am indebted to the many students and friends who urged me to write this second volume, but especially to the student teachers and alumni of St. Mary's School of Education, who field-tested these lessons and activities. I would like to thank Mike Kane, managing editor of the Innovative Division of Addison-Wesley, for his interest in this project when it was no more than an idea. For helping to clarify my explanations of scientific theories and concepts, I would like to thank the following scientists: Dr. Charles Higgins, Dr. Gyeong Soon Im, Dr. Tom Goodman, Dr. Lesley Higgins, and Dr. Phil Dauber. Priscilla Cox Samii, who served as the senior editor for both volumes, was not only extremely helpful, always available, and good humored, but brought a standard of excellence to the project that benefited both books. Above all, I am grateful for my patient and helpful husband, Bruce, whose encouragement enabled me to take the initiative and begin to write.

This book is published by Innovative Learning Publications™, an imprint of the Alternative Publishing Group of Addison-Wesley Publishing Company.

Managing Editor: Michael Kane
Project Editor: Priscilla Cox Samii
Production Director: Janet Yearian
Production Coordinator: Leanne Collins
Design Manager: Jeff Kelly
Text and Cover Design: Christy Butterfield
Illustrations and Cover Art: Kimberley Tolley

ISBN 0-201-45545-5

3 4 5 6 7 8 9 10-ML-98 97 96 95

Contents

Energy *125*
The Theme of Energy 126

Preface

What is the connection between art and science? Most people think of the artist and the scientist as living in completely separate worlds. The artist is often thought of as creative, intuitive, and somewhat disorganized, while the scientist is viewed as methodical, orderly, and somewhat calculating. Actually, many scientists bring artistry and creativity to their work, and many artists bring method and order to theirs.

Both scientists and artists have a great curiosity about the world around them. The scientist asks questions about the working of the natural world. The artist asks questions about the ways in which the world can be interpreted and re-created. In seeking answers, the artist uses the processes of perception, creation, and evaluation. The scientist uses the processes of observing, communicating, comparing, ordering, categorizing, relating, and inferring.

Art and science are two different ways of understanding and knowing the world around us. In some instances, the means of arriving at understanding are remarkably similar. Both the artist and the scientist are careful observers of natural phenomena. Both make comparisons of different forms, structures, and interactions, and both communicate and evaluate their findings. The scientist communicates through speaking and writing; the artist communicates through painting, drawing, sculpture, and other art media.

Meaningful art experiences help students develop skills related to creativity and problem solving. In our classrooms, we appreciate that speaking and writing are art forms that are studied in the works of great literature. The visual arts also have a language through which the artist speaks. Students must be given opportunities to understand this language and to learn to analyze what is communicated.

Through science, students can become captivated by the possibilities for discoveries in the natural world. The American poet Walt Whitman characterized science as a limitless voyage of joyous exploration. Exposure to hands-on science investigations provides students with opportunities to develop problem-solving and communication skills.

When students engage in activities that integrate art and science, they learn a variety of ways through which they can understand the world. They learn to bring creativity and insight to the discipline of science, and method and order to the discipline of art. Through the connection of art and science, students increase their appreciation of the natural world and develop an openness to the wonder and joy of life.

Introduction

The Art and Science Connection is a resource for the classroom
teacher or specialist interested in integrating art and science. The
lessons contained here have been field-tested by teachers in California
with students in regular, special education, and ESL (English as a
Second Language) classrooms.

The purpose of this curriculum is to provide students with a holistic,
hands-on approach to perceiving and learning about the natural world.
The lessons simultaneously engage students in the science processes of
observing, communicating, comparing, ordering, categorizing, relating
and inferring, and in the arts processes of perceiving, creating, and
evaluating.

Themes of Science

The American Association for the Advancement of Science (AAAS) has
recommended a major emphasis on themes in science curricula.
Thematic instruction reinforces the importance of understanding large,
overarching concepts rather than the memorization of isolated facts.

The investigations in these lessons are organized around three con-
ceptual themes: *structure, interactions,* and *energy.* These themes
are the overarching ideas that integrate the concepts of different
scientific disciplines, such as life science, earth science, and physical
science. They also integrate the elements and principles of the visual
arts and connect the concepts of science and art in meaningful ways.

Lesson Components

A typical lesson contains the following components:

Overview
A brief statement of the major focus, or theme, of the lesson.

Student Objectives
A listing of the learning and behavioral objectives embedded in the
lesson.

Materials
A list of materials and resources needed for the lesson.

Getting Ready
Step-by-step instructions for setting up demonstration and work areas.

Observing, Comparing, and Describing
Guidelines for a discussion in which students share their previous
knowledge about the concept(s) to be learned. The opening discussion
is usually followed by opportunities for observing, comparing, and
describing such natural phenomena as earthworms, ice cubes, or rocks.
In some lessons, observing is part of the creative process, as students
draw, paint, or sculpt from observation.

Drawing Conclusions

Suggestions for guiding students to share their observations and conclusions and to compare them with concepts they may have held previously. Occasionally this section includes additional information that may be provided by the teacher if appropriate.

Explaining the Phenomenon

Guidelines for an in-depth explanation of the concepts presented in the lesson. This section sometimes contains chemical or mathematical formulas that teachers may use to extend the understanding of middle school students.

Creating

Guidelines for a discussion and demonstration of media techniques introduced in the lesson, as well as suggestions to stimulate creative thinking. In this section of the lesson, students synthesize what they have learned about natural phenomena by creating a work of art.

Evaluating

Suggestions for guiding students to look critically at their own artwork. This is always a positive process. When evaluation consists of a whole-class discussion, input from individual students is voluntary.

Going Further

Suggestions for additional activities or sessions that extend the concepts introduced in the lesson or that connect the lesson with other areas of the curriculum.

Additional Resources

A list of resources useful in extending the lesson or in providing additional background information.

Background Information

Additional information for the teacher about the concepts introduced in the lesson. This section is not meant to be read aloud or reproduced for students.

Teaching the Lessons

Using the Lesson Format

The lessons contained in *The Art and Science Connection* are written in an organized, step-by-step format. No two classrooms are alike, however, in their interaction with the lesson content. Once a lesson has begun, students may ask questions or need more time on a particular activity. For this reason, the lesson format can only generalize what might occur in the lesson.

Time Frames

Since each classroom is unique, teachers will need to adapt the lessons to the needs of their own students. For some, a particular lesson might take 30 minutes, while for others the lesson is best divided into two sessions of 40 minutes each.

Using Cooperative Learning Strategies

All the lessons in *The Art and Science Connection* involve students in activities requiring some form of cooperative group work. If your students have had little experience with cooperative learning, you might wish to begin by having them work with a partner before moving to groups of three or four.

Introduce the idea of cooperative learning by having students talk about how they can help each other and cooperate on projects. Discuss the roles each individual will play in his or her group or pair. Provide modeling and practice so that students understand what cooperative learning looks and sounds like. Finally, after each cooperative learning lesson hold a short debriefing session to allow students to share ways in which they and their partners cooperated well.

A list of resources for cooperative learning can be found in the appendix on page 198.

Management and Planning

Tips for classroom management can be found on page 192 and include suggestions for effective planning, organization, and cleanup.

Structure

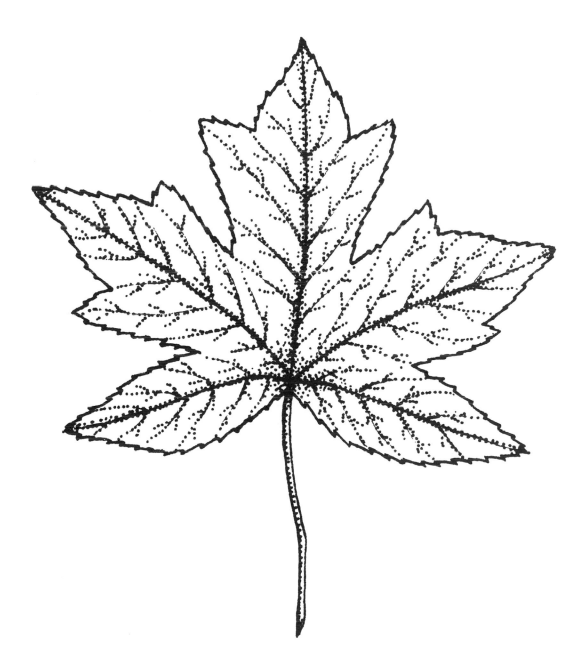

The Theme of Structure

The investigations in this section are organized around the theme of structure. In science, *structure* is defined as "the arrangement of particles or parts in a substance or body." Many kinds of structures are found in the natural world. A leaf, a planet, and an ice crystal each have a structure that can be observed and described. By investigating a variety of biological, physical, and geological forms, students discover how different structures are related.

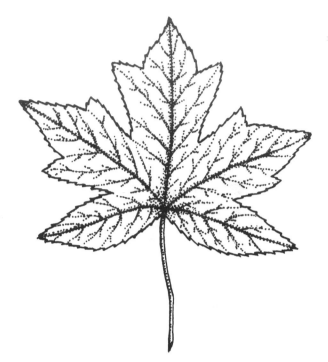

Structure at different levels of scale reveals different properties at each level. For instance, when first observing a leaf, students might notice its color, shape, stem, and veins. Observing a section of leaf under a microscope reveals an array of plant cells, each with its own microstructure. At another level, students might investigate a leaf as a part of the structure of a tree, which in turn forms part of the structure of a forest habitat.

Structure is an important theme in the visual arts, where it is defined as "a design or organization of independent parts to form a coordinated whole." This organization is achieved through the use of such visual elements as line, color, shape, and space, and such design principles as balance, symmetry, contrast, and repetition. The elements and principles of design contribute to the underlying structure of a work of art. When students are encouraged to notice the elements and principles of design in a painting, drawing, or sculpture, they learn to develop their aesthetic perception through awareness of structure.

Structure: "Describe It"

Overview

How can we describe and distinguish matter in its various forms? "Describe It!" is a game in which students learn to describe various objects and substances through close observation of such properties as size, weight, color, shape, and texture. Students can play "Describe It!" throughout the school year to sharpen their observations of various forms of plant and animal life, geological structures, machines, liquids, solids, and so on.

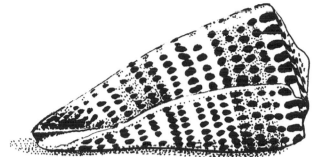

Student Objectives

- understand that all observable matter has properties that can be observed, described, and recorded.

- describe and compare the structure of various objects and substances through observation of such properties as size, weight, color, shape, and texture.

Materials

- 5–10 pairs of objects for students to describe, such as 2 twigs, rocks, shells, and jars of liquids

- (optional) sets of 3 objects, such as 3 leaves, bones, and feathers.

Getting Ready

Place the objects in a box so that students cannot view the contents.

note
Students should be organized into pairs.

Observing, Comparing, and Describing

1. Begin by having students share their knowledge of attributes. Hold up an object, such as a rock or shell, and ask students how it might be described. The following questions are useful in guiding discussion:

If you were to describe this object without naming it, what words might you use to indicate its size? *(tiny, small, large, enormous, 12 inches long, as big as an egg, etc.)*

What words might you use to indicate its probable weight? *(heavy as a softball, about 1 pound, etc.)*

What words might you use to indicate its texture? *(soft, hard, rough, smooth, etc.)*

What words might you use to indicate its color and shape? *(Answers will vary.)*

2. Explain that the words listed on the board are the *properties*, or attributes, of the object. All *matter*, the stuff of which our observable universe is made, can be described by its properties.

3. Tell students that they will play a game to sharpen their observation skills. They will also strengthen their ability to *discriminate,* to perceive the distinguishing properties of one object or substance that make it different from another.

4. Explain the rules:

One student is the presenter, and the rest of the students play with a partner. Partners sit face to face; one faces the presenter, and the other sits with his or her back to the presenter.

The student facing the presenter takes the role of the speaker, and the student with his or her back to the presenter takes the role of the listener.

When partners are in position, the presenter holds up an object for the speakers to observe in silence for several minutes. Listeners cannot see the object, because they are facing the opposite direction.

When the presenter says, "Describe it!" speakers describe the object's structure to their partners. *Speakers can neither say what the object is, nor mention its function.* Listeners may not ask questions.

After several minutes, the presenter says, "Stop!" and hides the object. Listeners then turn to face the presenter.

The presenter next holds up two objects for all to see—the object the presenter had previously shown the speakers and a very similar object.

The presenter then asks the listeners to guess, based on the descriptions given by their partners, which of the two objects the speakers were describing. Listeners show their guesses by holding up one finger if they guess the first object, and two fingers if they guess the second.

The presenter reveals the correct object. Listeners and speakers then exchange roles and positions and play another round.

5. Model the game by playing a practice round with two students as the rest of the class watches.

6. When students understand the procedure, begin the game. After you have played several rounds, select a student to be the presenter for the next round. You may increase the difficulty of the game by using three rather than two objects.

note

When first playing the game, *you* should take the role of presenter.

Evaluating

At the end of each round, ask the listeners, "What did your partner say about this object that helped you guess correctly?" Ask the speakers, "Is there anything you might do differently next time?"

Going Further

Have students generate a list of questions for further investigation. Examples of such questions are:

What other kinds of objects can be observed and described? Bring art prints or slides to class. Help students observe and describe the structure of paintings, drawings, and sculptures. The following questions are useful in guiding students' perception:

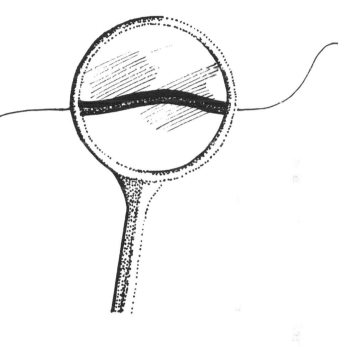

> What kinds of lines do you see?
>
> What kinds of shapes?
>
> What colors has the artist used?
>
> How would you describe the texture of this artwork?
>
> Can you find any repetition of line, shape, or color?

How can forms that are too small to be seen with the naked eye be observed and described? Have students use hand lenses or microscopes to examine and compare pieces of leaves, bones, feathers, onion skin, and so on.

Additional Resources

Alexander, Kay. "Developing Aesthetic Perception," in *Learning to Look and Create: The Spectra Program.* Palo Alto, Calif.: Dale Seymour, 1987.

Lowery, Larry. "Inorganic Matter," in *The Everyday Science Sourcebook.* Palo Alto, Calif.: Dale Seymour, 1985.

Solids

Overview

What is a solid? How does its structure affect its
hardness and flexibility? Students compare and rank a
collection of solids according to their degree of hardness,
flexibility, and adhesiveness. They observe the
properties of such art materials as graphite pencil, chalk,
charcoal, and wax crayon. Finally, students use the
properties of solids to create a mixed-media drawing
with art chalk and wax crayon.

Student Objectives

- observe that a solid tends to keep its shape when it is
  left alone.

- observe that not all solids have the same structure.
  Some are harder or more flexible or more adhesive
  than others.

- use two solid materials—chalk and wax crayon—in creating a mixed-
  media drawing.

Materials

- collections of 10 solid objects, such as a rock, ball of modeling clay, stick
  of chalk, crayon, stick of charcoal, rubber band, paper clip, facial tissue,
  and glass jar, 1 collection per group of 4 students

- containers to hold solid objects, such as tubs or shoe boxes, 1 per group
  of 4 students

- Logsheet 1: Investigating Solids (page 162)

- straight pins

- pennies

- pencils and erasers

- white drawing paper, 5 per group of 4 students, and 1 for the teacher

- newspapers to cover work areas

- facial tissues

- art chalk in assorted colors

- wax crayons in dark colors, such as black, dark blue, green, purple, and
  red

- paper towels

- water

Getting Ready

1. Organize collections of solid objects into tubs or other containers. You will need ten different solid objects for each group of four students. Arrange one collection of solid objects on a table near the front of the classroom where everyone can see it.

2. For each group of four students, organize the following materials for easy distribution during the "Observing, Describing, and Comparing" portion of the lesson: one collection of solids, logsheets, four straight pins, four pennies, one sheet of drawing paper, and four pencils with erasers.

3. Cover work areas with newspaper.

4. Dampen some paper towels with water. Arrange the drawing paper, facial tissues, art chalk, crayons, and damp paper towels for easy distribution during the "Creating" portion of the lesson.

note
Students should be organized into groups of four.

Observing, Comparing, and Describing

1. Begin by having students share their knowledge of solids. The following questions are useful in guiding discussion:

What do the expressions "rock solid" and "frozen solid" mean? *(Extremely hard or durable; immovable)*

How does a solid differ from a liquid? *(A solid keeps its shape when left alone; a liquid flows.)*

What are some of the solids in this classroom? *(Answers will vary. Examples: chair, desk.)*

What solid substances have you eaten in the past 24 hours? *(Answers will vary. Examples: apple, bread.)*

2. Tell students that a *solid* is a substance that keeps its shape when it is left alone. Explain that not all solids have the same properties. Some solids are rigid, while others are flexible. Some are soft, while others are hard, or smooth, or crumbly, and so on.

3. Tell students that they will work in groups of four to investigate a collection of solid objects. Explain that they will *rank,* or order, solids according to such attributes as hardness, flexibility, and adhesiveness.

4. Distribute copies of Logsheet 1: Investigating Solids. Tell students that as they complete the logsheet, each person should share ideas and observations with others in the group.

5. Demonstrate the procedure:

First, test each solid for *hardness.* Order the solids according to degree of hardness. Record the ranking on the logsheet by writing the names of the solids in order from very soft to very hard. Use the criteria that follow.

very soft	can be scratched with a fingernail
soft	can be scratched with the edge of a penny
hard	can be scratched with a straight pin
very hard	cannot be scratched at all

Second, test each solid for *flexibility*. Order the solids according to degree of flexibility. Record the ranking on the logsheet. Use the following criteria:

very flexible	bends easily in any direction
less flexible	bends with some difficulty
very rigid	cannot bend at all

Third, test each solid for *adhesiveness*—its ability to stick to paper. Order the solids according to their degree of adhesiveness. Record the ranking on the logsheet. To test a solid, rub it against a sheet of drawing paper. Use the following criteria:

very adhesive	leaves a mark on the paper that is difficult to rub off
less adhesive	leaves a mark on the paper that rubs off fairly easily
nonadhesive	leaves no mark on the paper

6. When students understand the procedure, distribute the materials and have them begin. Circulate, and offer assistance as needed.

Drawing Conclusions

Gather students together to discuss the results. Have a member of each group share the group's rankings. The following questions are useful in guiding discussion:

How did your group rank each solid according to hardness, flexibility, and adhesiveness? *(Answers may vary, depending on the solid materials used.)*

How were the solids in the collection similar? *(Each kept its shape when left alone.)*

How did the solids differ? *(They differed in degrees of hardness, flexibility, and adhesiveness.)*

How could some of these solids be liquified, or turned into liquids? *(By heating to the melting point)*

Explaining the Phenomenon

Matter on earth exists in three forms: as a solid, a liquid, or a gas. All matter is composed of smaller units called *atoms* or *molecules*. The atoms or molecules of a solid are in fixed positions. In other words, they stay in place with respect to their nearby neighbors. They move about somewhat, but they don't change places. If they did, they would flow, changing the solid into a liquid.

When exposed to extreme temperatures, the atoms or molecules of a solid become excited. They move about faster and faster until the bonds holding them together break, changing the solid into a liquid state.

The arrangement of the atoms and molecules in a solid forms its structure. The structure of a solid determines whether it is hard or soft, rigid or flexible, and so on. In diamond, the hardest mineral known, carbon atoms are held together in a rigid, closely packed pattern by strong bonds in various directions. Graphite, which forms pencil lead, is also made of carbon atoms. However, in graphite, the atoms are bound together with strong bonds only in a single plane. This arrangement allows sheets of graphite to break and slide apart, depositing some graphite on the paper when you write or draw.

note

For more information about atoms and molecules, see "Atoms and Molecules: Background Information" on page 11.

Creating

1. Tell students that artists make use of solids that adhere to paper. Examples of such solids include pencils, charcoal, crayons, and chalk. Tell students that next they will make drawings that use two solids: chalk and crayon.

2. Demonstrate how to hold a piece of chalk on its side and rub it back and forth over an area of the paper that is roughly the size of your hand.

3. Take another color and rub an area next to the first. Continue using different pieces of chalk until the entire paper is covered with different patches of color.

4. Take a facial tissue and rub the chalk surface to blend the edges of the colored areas together. Move the tissue in a circular motion as you go over the paper.

5. Explain that the chalk can be blended and smudged with the tissue because it does not stick well to the paper's surface. Have students observe the chalk on your fingers, and point out that their hands will become stained as well. Explain that they should not worry, because the chalk will wipe off easily later with a damp paper towel.

6. Show students the colored chalk background you have made, and ask what it reminds them of. Perhaps it reminds them of flowers or the sea.

note

Roll up your sleeves before you start, and have your students do the same before they begin to use the chalk. Explain that they should try not to touch their clothes as they work. Remind them that because chalk does not stick very well to things, it will rub off easily on paper, hands, and clothes.

7. Take a black or other dark wax crayon, and explain that you now will draw over the chalk background with the wax crayon. Tell students that if the background makes them think of the sea, they might draw different kinds of fish swimming. Or, they might draw flowers or buildings. Have students share as many ideas as possible at this stage.

8. Using the crayon, draw a picture over the background. Leave spaces between your lines so that the background comes through.

9. When students understand the procedure, distribute the materials and have them begin. Circulate, and offer assistance when necessary.

Evaluating

1. Display the finished drawings for everyone to see. Ask students to identify examples of blending—where the artist used tissue to smooth the chalk.

2. Ask volunteers to share one thing they like about their own or a classmate's drawing.

Going Further

Have students generate a list of questions for further investigation. Examples of such questions are:

- *How else can solids be compared?* Have students compare the weights of different solids. Given a collection of solid items, students can predict the weights by ordering the items serially—for example, from heaviest to lightest. Next, students can use a balance scale to test their predictions.

  Students can also compare the volumes of different solid objects. Have students immerse a variety of nonabsorbent solids into a graduated cylinder. Each submerged object will raise the water level as it displaces an equal volume of water. By finding the difference between the initial water level and the raised water level, students can calculate the volume of the object in cubic centimeters. Students may record these measurements in a journal or logbook.

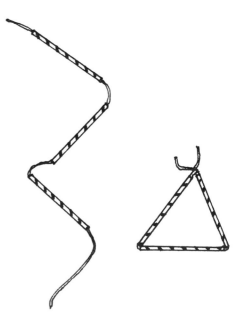

- *What kinds of atomic or molecular structures are the strongest?* Students can create models to simulate the structures of atomic or molecular bonds in solids. Have students feed some string through three drinking straws. Then have them bring the ends together and tie a knot, making sure the ends of the straws touch and form a triangle. Students can do the same with four straws (square), and six straws (hexagon). Tell them to pull and push on the straw shapes. Students will notice that the triangular shape is the only rigid framework.

Additional Resources

Berger, Melvin. *Atoms, Molecules, and Quarks.* New York: Putnam, 1986.

Lowery, Lawrence F. "Solids," in *The Everyday Science Sourcebook.* Palo Alto, Calif.: Dale Seymour, 1985.

• •

Atoms and Molecules: Background Information

More than 2000 years ago, Greek philosophers, including Democritus and Leucippus (approximately 400 B.C.), believed that every substance was made of invisible units that could not be broken or divided. They called these tiny units *atoms.* It was only near the end of the 19th century that experiments began to show the nature of atoms and the structures they build, which we call *molecules.*

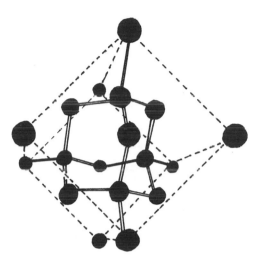

Diamond structure

How big is an atom? You can rub a tiny piece of soot (carbon) from a campfire between your fingers until it disappears in a layer too thin to be seen by the naked eye. Carbon atoms are a little more than 1×10^{-8} cm across, and the diameters of even the largest atoms are only three times larger. If you could count the atoms that lie side by side along a centimeter of a pencil lead, there would be 100 million.

Atoms often join into bundles called *molecules* that have their own chemical identities. Water is an example of matter that is composed of molecules. A water molecule is composed of two hydrogen atoms bound to an oxygen atom. The bond between these atoms is so strong that they will separate only under extreme conditions.

Molecules sometimes are attracted to each other. The attraction between molecules of the same kind is called *cohesion,* and the attraction between molecules of a different kind is called *adhesion.* Various kinds of bonds hold different atoms or molecules together. When any two neutral atoms or molecules come close together, weak bonds occur, called *van der Waals bonds.* These bonds may form when two atoms have oppositely charged regions facing each other that come close together, giving rise to an attraction.

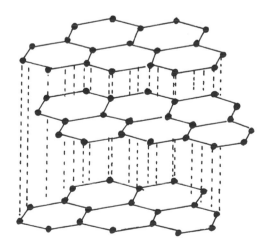

Graphite structure

In any solid, the atoms or molecules are in relatively fixed positions. When a repeating pattern exists in the placement of the atoms or molecules throughout the solid, it is called *crystalline.* If the atoms or molecules have no particular arrangement, the solid is called *amorphous.* How these atoms or molecules are arranged determines the strength, or hardness, of a solid. For instance, both diamond and graphite are pure forms of carbon. The atoms in a diamond structure are in a closely packed pattern, held rigid by bonds pointing at various angles in all three dimensions. In graphite, strong bonds bind the atoms together in sheets. These sheets are held together by weaker attractions between the planes, so the individual sheets of atoms can easily slip past each other.

Liquids

Overview

What is a liquid? Students compare four liquids—catsup, syrup, water, and milk. They observe that liquids differ in appearance, odor, and texture. They rank the four liquids according to their degree of viscosity and weight. Finally, students use the properties of liquids to create free-flowing designs with tempera paint.

Student Objectives

- compare four liquids by appearance, odor, texture, and viscosity.

- use a balance scale to rank equal volumes of liquids according to weight.

- create abstract designs by blowing tempera paint across paper.

Materials

- small containers, each identical, such as paper or plastic cups, 8 per group of 4 students

- catsup, 2 cups

- corn syrup or honey, 2 cups

- water

- milk, 2 cups

- measuring cup

- balance scales, 1 per group of 4 students

- Logsheet 2: Comparing Liquids (page 163)

- pencils

- watches with second hands, 1 per group

- paper towels

- newspapers to cover work areas

- containers, such as cut-off milk cartons or plastic cups, 5 per group of 4 students

- liquid tempera paint, assorted colors

- plastic teaspoons, 1 per container of tempera paint

- drinking straws

- construction paper, white, 18" x 24"

Getting Ready

1. For each group of four students, prepare the following set of materials: one container each of 1/4 cup of catsup, syrup, water, and milk; four empty containers; one balance scale; logsheets, pencils; and a set of damp and dry paper towels. Organize these materials for easy distribution during the "Observing, Comparing, and Describing" portion of the activity.

2. Cover work areas with newspaper.

3. Prepare a container of water and four containers of tempera paint, each a different color, for each group of four students. Dilute the paint with water until its consistency is like that of food coloring or ink. Place a plastic teaspoon in each container. Organize the containers, straws, and white paper for easy distribution during the "Creating" portion of the activity.

4. Set aside a place in the classroom where finished paintings can be laid flat to dry.

Observing, Comparing, and Describing

1. Begin by having students share their knowledge of liquids. The following questions are useful in guiding discussion:

How does a liquid differ from a solid? *(A solid keeps its shape when left alone; a liquid flows.)*

What are some of the liquids in this classroom? *(Water, glue, paint, ink, etc.)*

What liquid substances have you consumed in the past 24 hours? *(Answers will vary. Examples: milk, water.)*

2. Explain that a *liquid* is a substance that flows. The molecules of a liquid are close enough to touch, as are those of a solid, but the molecules of a liquid attract each other with weaker forces than do those of a solid.

3. Tell students that they will work in groups of four to investigate four liquids: catsup, syrup, water, and milk.

4. Distribute copies of Logsheet 2: Comparing Liquids. Tell students that as they complete the logsheet, each person should share ideas and observations with others in the group.

5. Demonstrate the procedure:

First, notice the *physical appearance* of each liquid. What color is it? Is it clear or opaque? Record your group's observations on the logsheet.

note
Students should be organized into groups of four.

Second, smell each liquid. What is its *odor*? Is it sweet or acrid? Musty or neutral? Record your group's observations.

Third, place your fingers into each liquid to discover its *texture*, the way it feels. Is it slippery or sticky? Smooth or grainy? Record your group's observations.

Fourth, use a balance scale to compare the liquids by *weight*. Rank the liquids according to which is heaviest, second heaviest, third heaviest, and so on. Record the rankings on the logsheet.

Finally, pour each liquid into an empty container and count, in seconds, how long it takes for most of the liquid to pour out. The longer it takes, the greater the liquid's *viscosity*, or thickness. Rank the liquids on the logsheet from thick to thin.

6. When students understand the procedure, distribute the materials and have them begin. Circulate, and offer assistance as needed.

catsup

We noticed that catsup is dark red-brown. It is opaque and smells sweet and musty.

SAFETY TIP
Caution students against tasting any of the liquids.

Drawing Conclusions

Gather students together to discuss the results. Have a member of each group share the group's descriptions and rankings. The following questions are useful in guiding discussion:

How did your group describe each liquid's appearance, odor, and texture? *(Answers may vary somewhat.)*

How did your group rank each liquid according to weight? *(Probably syrup was heaviest, followed by catsup, milk, and water; answers may vary, depending on the kind of syrup or catsup used.)*

How did your group rank each liquid according to viscosity? *(Probably catsup was most viscous, followed by syrup, milk, and water.)*

How were the liquids in the collection similar? *(Each flowed; each assumed the shape of its container.)*

How could some of these liquids be solidified, or turned into solids? *(By freezing; by allowing the water to evaporate from some mixtures and solutions)*

Explaining the Phenomenon

Matter on earth exists in three forms: as a solid, a liquid, or a gas. All matter is composed of smaller units called *atoms* or *molecules*. The atoms or molecules of a *liquid* are held together with weaker forces than those of a solid. This is why a liquid will flow and assume the shape of whatever container it is in.

The arrangement of atoms or molecules in a liquid forms its structure. The structure of a liquid determines whether it is slippery or sticky, light or heavy, or thick or thin.

When you pour syrup from a bottle, you may notice that the syrup flows more slowly near the rim of the bottle mouth than in the center of the stream. This is because the molecules at the surface of a solid don't move, and any liquid molecules pressed against them won't move easily either. You can observe the same effect if you press your hand hard against your thigh and then try to move it sideways. Your hand will be held in place by frictional forces acting between your hand and your thigh. The *frictional forces* acting between the surface of the glass bottle and the liquid slow the movement of the molecules nearest the glass surface.

As the molecules within a liquid flow, they attract and collide with each other. The attraction and collision interfere with the liquid's ability to flow easily. This internal friction is called *viscosity*. Some liquids, such as molasses and syrup, have a greater viscosity than others, such as alcohol or water. Other liquids, such as toothpaste, are so viscous that they hardly seem to flow at all.

Creating

1. Tell students that artists use the properties of liquids to create a variety of abstract effects in paintings. Explain that they will next experiment to create different designs by making liquid tempera paint flow across paper.

2. Demonstrate the procedure:

Use a teaspoon to place a small puddle of tempera paint on the paper.

Use a straw to blow the paint across the surface. Blow the paint as far as you can without going off the paper.

Rotate the paper to change the direction of the paint as you blow.

Repeat the procedure with different colors.

Experiment with adding a teaspoonful of water to the paper and blowing it across the wet paint.

Experiment with blowing colors across each other. Continue until the paper is covered with a web of color.

3. When students understand the procedure, distribute the materials and have them begin. Encourage students to fill the page as completely as they can. Circulate, and offer assistance as needed.

Evaluating

Display the finished paintings for everyone to see. Ask students to compare the different kinds of effects created by their classmates. The following questions are useful in guiding discussion:

Can you identify examples of a color flowing into or over another color?

What kinds of effects were created when water flowed into or over paint? Can you find examples of this technique?

note

For more information, see "Atoms and Molecules: Background Information" on page 11.

note

Point out that continuous blowing may leave students short of breath. Tell them to stop for a while if they begin to feel dizzy.

note

You may extend the art activity by having students create a collage with pieces of paper torn from their straw-blown designs. The torn papers may be mounted with contrasting pieces of paper in solid colors.

What effects were created by a steady, slowly flowing stream of paint? By a quickly flowing stream?

Going Further

Have students generate a list of questions for further investigation. Examples of such questions are:

- *How is water important in the processes of the artist?* Have students work in groups to investigate art techniques that make use of water, such as watercolor and tempera painting, sculpting with ceramic clay, papier mâché, pen-and-ink drawing, and so on. Students can also experiment to discover which art materials dissolve in water. Many art materials are soluble in water, making water, the universal solvent, an ideal medium for cleaning up messy art projects.

- *What are other properties of liquids?* Students can investigate the buoyant properties of water. Have them fill a container to the brim with water and place a toy boat on the surface, catching the overflow with another container. When they weigh the overflow, students will discover that the weight of the displaced water is equal to the boat's own weight.

Additional Resources

Agler, Leigh. *Liquid Explorations.* Berkeley, Calif.: Lawrence Hall of Science, University of California, 1987.

Elementary Science Study: Drops, Streams, and Containers. Hudson, N.H.: Delta Education, 1986.

Surface Tension

Overview

What is the structure of water? In this investigation, students discover the properties of surface tension. They experiment to discover how many water drops can fit on the surface of a penny. They observe that soap interacts with water to destroy surface tension. As artists, students then use the interaction of soap and water to create swirling abstract designs with milk, liquid detergent, and food colors.

Student Objectives

- experiment to discover how many water drops can fit on the surface of a penny.

- observe that soap destroys the surface tension of water.

- use milk, liquid detergent, and food colors to create an abstract design with a strong color emphasis.

Materials

- containers, such as cut-off milk cartons or plastic cups, 8 per group of 4 students

- droppers or straws

- liquid detergent, about 2 cups

- pennies

- paper towels

- milk, 1/2 gallon

- brushes

- food coloring, 1 bottle each of red, blue, yellow

- white construction paper, 9" x 12"

- newspapers

- water

Getting Ready

1. For each group of four students, fill two water containers with 1/2 cup of water. Place four droppers or straws into each container. Fill one container with 1/4 cup of liquid detergent.

2. Organize water containers, detergent containers, pennies, and paper towels for easy distribution during the "Observing, Comparing, and Describing" portion of the lesson.

3. For each group of four students, fill two containers each with 1/2 cup of milk. Place two brushes in each container of milk. Into three containers put two tablespoons of food colors—one color per container: red, blue, and yellow.

4. Organize milk containers, brushes, food colors, and construction paper for easy distribution during the "Creating" portion of the lesson.

5. Cover work areas with newspaper.

6. Set aside an area of the classroom where finished paintings can be laid flat to dry.

note

Students should be organized into groups of four.

Observing, Comparing, and Describing

1. Begin by having students share their knowledge of water's properties. The following questions are useful in guiding discussion:

What is water? *(A liquid composed of water molecules)*

How can we describe water? *(It flows, is usually clear, changes state from solid to liquid to gas, sticks to some things but not to others; its surface forms a very thin skin; etc.)*

What is water made of? *(Each water molecule is composed of two hydrogen atoms and one oxygen atom.)*

2. Distribute a penny, water container, and dropper (or straw) to each student. Have students place one drop of water on the surface of a penny.

note

If you are using straws instead of eyedroppers, show students how to use a straw to release a drop of water (see "Tips for Working with Science Materials" on page 195).

3. Ask students to describe the water drop in as much detail as possible. *(It forms a dome, is clear, acts to magnify the surface of the penny, etc.)*

4. Ask students to predict how many water drops will fit on the surface of a penny without running over the edge. Allow time for students to discuss their predictions with others in their groups. Record the range of predictions on the chalkboard.

5. Tell students to carefully add 1 drop of water at a time to the surface of a penny until the water runs off the edge. Ask them to observe periodically the penny from the side to see whether its dome shape is changing in any way.

6. When students understand the procedure, have them begin. Circulate, and offer assistance as needed. Students who finish early can dry their pennies and try again.

7. After everyone has finished the experiment, have students share their results. (Many students will have been able to place more than 40 drops on the surface of the penny.) Ask students to describe the appearance of the water on the penny as they added more drops. (The dome grew larger, bulging upward and outward.)

8. Tell students that next they will add 5 drops of liquid detergent to their water container, thoroughly stir, and repeat the experiment using the water and soap solution. Ask students to predict the number of drops they will be able to place on the penny. Allow time for students to discuss and share their predictions.

9. Remind students to view periodically the penny from the side as they add drops during the second experiment. When students understand the procedure, have them begin.

Drawing Conclusions

Have students discuss their results and observations. The following questions are useful in guiding discussion:

What was the difference in the number of drops you added to the penny during the second experiment? *(Answers will vary.)*

How did the water on the penny appear during the first experiment? *(As a bulging dome)* During the second experiment? *(Flat and spreading toward the edge)*

Explaining the Phenomenon

Water is composed of water molecules, small units that consist of two atoms of hydrogen and one atom of oxygen. The two hydrogen atoms stick out of the water molecule like Mickey Mouse ears.

Water is held together by the attraction of its molecules for one another. Some of these attractive forces are called *bonds*. The two hydrogen atoms in each water molecule are highly active, charged bodies that grab at and hold on to the oxygen atom of other water molecules. Thus, the molecules of water are continuously pulling on each other.

An invisible skin forms on the surface of water because of the attractions of its molecules for each other. This property of water is called *surface tension*. Surface tension causes a water drop to form a bulge, or dome.

The molecules of soap are very attracted to the molecules of water. When soap comes into contact with water, its molecules form a bond with the water's molecules. This bond changes the way the water molecules are arranged. The tight bonds between the water molecules are replaced by a looser arrangement of soap and water molecules.

When liquid detergent is added to water, the new arrangement of soap and water molecules causes the surface tension of the water to loosen and break apart. The drops of soapy water do not have sufficiently strong bonds at their surface to form a skin capable of holding a large quantity of water on a penny.

note
For more information on atoms and molecules, see "Atoms and Molecules: Background Information" on page 11.

Creating

1. Tell students that artists can make use of the interaction of water and soap molecules to create abstract designs.

2. Demonstrate the procedure:

Dip a bristle brush into a container of milk. Cover the surface of a sheet of 9" x 12" white construction paper with a layer of milk.

Use the brush to dab a thick puddle of milk onto the center of the wet paper. The puddle should be about 3 inches wide.

Use droppers (or straws) to place 2 or more drops of different food colors on the surface of the puddle. The drops should be at least 1 inch apart.

Use a dropper to place a small drop of liquid detergent in the center of each drop of food coloring. As the soap molecules attach themselves to the water molecules in the food coloring, the colors will spread out across the milk and form streams of color that mix and twist across the paper.

note
Inform students that food coloring will stain hands and clothing. Remind them to work carefully to avoid spillage.

3. Tell students that as they create different designs using milk, detergent, and food colors, they should try to achieve a feeling of color emphasis in each design. Explain that *emphasis* is the dominance of one part of a design in relation to other parts. To create color emphasis, one color should stand out from the rest in the finished design.

4. When students understand the procedure, distribute the materials and have them begin. Circulate, and offer assistance as needed. Encourage students to emphasize one color over the others in each of their designs.

Evaluating

Display the finished designs for everyone to see. Have students notice and compare the emphasis achieved by their classmates in each design.

Going Further

Have students generate a list of questions for further investigation. Examples of such questions are:

- *What kinds of objects can float on water's skin?* Students can investigate the strength of water's surface tension. Have them fill a shallow pan with water and attempt to float such items as metal paper clips and sewing pins on its surface.

- *Do other substances loosen water's surface tension?* Have students repeat the penny experiment, placing as many water drops on the surface of a penny as they can. Then, have them repeat the experiment using drops of such solutions as sugar water, salt water, and so on. Have them record their observations in a journal or logbook.

Number of drops	Substances
25	water
16	alcohol
	sugar water

Additional Resources

Agler, Leigh. *Liquid Explorations.* Berkeley, Calif.: Lawrence Hall of Science, University of California, 1987.

Allison, Linda, and David Katz. "Water's Weird Skin: Testing Surface Tension," in *Gee, Wiz!* Boston: Little, Brown, 1983.

Elementary Science Study: Drops, Streams, and Containers. Hudson, N.H.: Delta Education, 1986.

Loam and Clay

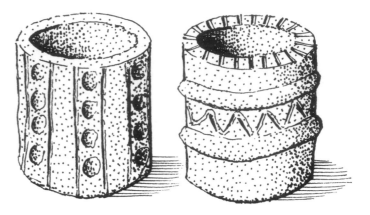

Overview

What is soil? In this activity, students identify and compare the properties of loam (garden soil) and clay. As artists, they then use modeling techniques to craft a textured pot from ceramic clay.

Student Objectives

- identify the ingredients of loam, or garden soil.

- compare the properties of loam and clay.

- use modeling techniques to craft a textured pot from ceramic clay.

Materials

- garden soil, 1 trowelful per group of 4 students

- bucket or other large container to hold soil

- trowel or large spoon

- newspapers

- ceramic clay, one 25-lb bag for each 20 students

- sturdy wire, 2-ft length

- plastic wrap

- hand lenses

- scissors

- paper clips, opened

- Logsheet 3: Comparing Loam and Clay (page 164)

- individual place mats for work areas, such as oilcloth or fabric-backed wallpaper samples

- wax paper

- frozen juice containers

- objects for impressing textures, such as toothpicks, forks, and paper clips

- kiln

- (optional) glazes

Getting Ready

1. Obtain some garden soil, either from your own garden or from a local nursery. You will need one trowelful for each group of four students.

Place the loam in a bucket or other large container with a trowel or large spoon.

2. Cover work areas with newspaper.

3. Use a length of wire to cut ceramic clay into slabs at least 1/2" thick, one slab for each student. Cover the slabs with plastic wrap to keep them moist until ready for use. For each group of four students, prepare one egg-sized lump of clay and cover it with plastic wrap.

4. Organize hand lenses, loam, clay eggs, and logsheets for easy distribution during the "Observing, Comparing, and Describing" portion of the lesson.

5. Organize place mats, clay slabs, wax paper sheets, juice cans, and objects for impressing textures for easy distribution during the "Creating" portion of the lesson.

6. Set aside an area of the classroom where the clay pots can dry for 2 or 3 weeks.

note
Students should be organized into groups of four.

Observing, Comparing, and Describing

1. Begin by having students share their knowledge of soil. The following questions are useful in guiding discussion:

What is soil made of? *(Small particles of rock, plant materials, etc.)*

Where is soil found? *(Where rocks have worn away; where plants grow; in fields, gardens, etc.)*

How is soil made? *(By the wearing away of rocks and sand and by the decomposition of plant and animal materials)*

2. Hold up a handful or trowelful of garden soil for students to see. Tell students that they will work in groups to examine a small amount of garden soil, or *loam*, to identify its ingredients.

3. Hold up an egg-sized portion of ceramic clay. Tell students that they will also examine another type of soil, called *clay*, to identify its ingredients and compare it with the loam.

4. Distribute copies of Logsheet 3: Comparing Loam and Clay. Tell students that as they each complete the logsheet, they should share ideas and observations with others in the group.

5. Demonstrate the procedure:

Spread the loam over an area of newspaper. Examine the loam with a hand lens. Notice what the loam is made of. Observe its appearance, odor, and texture.

On the logsheet, list the things you find in the loam. Write a thorough description of the loam's appearance, odor, and texture. Then quickly sketch each kind of item you find.

Take a piece of clay and spread it thinly over another area of newspaper. Closely examine the clay with a hand lens. Notice what the clay is made of. Notice its appearance, odor, and texture.

On the logsheet, list the things you find in the clay, and describe the clay thoroughly. Sketch each kind of item you find.

6. When students understand the procedure, distribute a trowelful of loam, a clay egg, and four hand lenses to each group. Have students begin recording their observations. Circulate, and offer assistance as needed.

Drawing Conclusions

Have a member from each group share conclusions. The following questions are useful in guiding discussion:

What kinds of things did your group find in the loam? *(Small particles of rocks, sand, wood, leaves, insects, etc.)*

What kinds of things did your group find in the clay? *(Tiny particles of rock)*

How do the loam and clay differ? *(The loam is loosely packed and does not easily stick together or to other things; the clay is densely packed and sticks to itself and to other things.)*

Explaining the Phenomenon

Soil is made by the weathering and wearing away, or *erosion*, of rocks. Soil is composed of tiny particles of rocks and minerals and bits of decayed plant and animal matter.

Clay is soil that is made up almost entirely of tiny rock and mineral particles. When moistened with water, clay particles stick tightly together. Most plants have difficulty growing in clay soils because there are so few air spaces between the densely packed clay particles.

Loam is soil that is made up of clay, sand, and *organic matter,* or bits of decayed plant and animal materials. Loam contains particles of varying sizes loosely packed together. Most plants grow well in loam because the loose arrangement of the loam particles allows air spaces to form.

Creating

1. Tell students that artists and craftspeople use clay to create sculptures and such household items as vases, pots, and dishes. The flexibility of clay makes it easy to shape into various forms. Explain that they will use clay to create a small pot.

2. Demonstrate the procedure:

Wrap a piece of wax paper around a juice can to determine its circumference. Trim the paper to exactly cover the circumference of the can.

Lay the paper rectangle on the clay slab. Use an opened paper clip to cut out the clay around the rectangle.

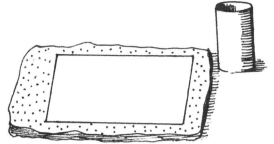

Wrap the wax paper around the juice can. Cover the wax paper with the clay rectangle. Use the paper clip to score (roughen) the edges of the clay, then moisten them slightly and press them together. Smooth the surface to conceal the weld.

Place the clay-covered can on top of another slab of clay. Use the paper clip to trace around the base and cut out a circular piece for the bottom. Join the bottom piece to the pot by scoring, moistening, and pressing the clay edges together.

Carefully extract the juice can from the clay. Remove the wax paper.

Seal any cracks in the pot by smoothing the clay together with your fingers. Smooth the entire surface of the pot.

Use a variety of tools—toothpicks, forks, paper clips, and so on—to create textures and patterns on the surface of the pot. Press gently when applying texture so as not to distort the shape of the pot.

Scratch your initials on the bottom of the pot.

3. When students understand the procedure, distribute the art materials and have them begin. Circulate, and offer assistance as needed.

4. When the pots are finished, place them on a counter or shelf and cover them with plastic wrap to slow the drying process. Allow the pots to dry for 2 or 3 weeks before firing in a kiln to cone .05.

Final Touches

Students may wish to glaze their pots. The pots may be covered with glaze after the first firing. Caution students against placing any glaze on the bottom of the pot. Do not let the pots touch one another in the kiln during the second firing.

Evaluating

Display the finished pots for everyone to see. Have students compare the textural effects created by their classmates. Ask them to identify textures that appear rough, prickly, bumpy, smooth, and so on.

Going Further

Have students generate a list of questions for further investigation. Examples of such questions are:

■ *How is soil formed?* Students can observe the weathering and wearing of rocks into smaller particles that make up soils. Have students rub various kinds of rocks together over a sheet of black paper and observe the small particles that fall onto the paper. Wind and water carry abrasive materials that wear away rocks in a similar way. Take students outdoors to find places where plants have grown up through concrete or asphalt, causing it to crack and wear away.

- *How does soil influence the growth of plants?* Students can compare the growth of plants in various soils. Fill one planting container with sand, another with clay, and a third with loam. Plant several lima bean seeds in each container and place the containers where they will receive equal amounts of light and water. Have students keep a record of the beans' growth for a month. Students may record their observations and conclusions in a journal or logbook.

Additional Resources

Alexander, Kay. "Folk Artists," in *Learning to Look and Create: The Spectra Program, Grade Five.* Palo Alto, Calif.: Dale Seymour, 1988.

Fodor, R. V. *Chiseling the Earth: How Erosion Shapes the Land.* Hillside, N.J.: Enslow, 1983.

Lowery, Larry. "Inorganic Matter," in *The Everyday Science Sourcebook.* Palo Alto, Calif.: Dale Seymour, 1985.

Backyard Creatures

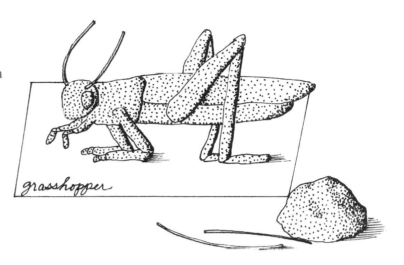

grasshopper

Overview

What variations in structure can we observe in the animals that inhabit our backyards? In this activity, students get a firsthand look at the incredible diversity of animal life. They compare the external structure of animals from three phyla: snails (Phylum Mollusca), earthworms (Phylum Annelida), and insects (Phylum Arthropoda). As artists, they use modeling clay to create a realistic three-dimensional representation of one or more animals.

Student Objectives

- observe and compare the external structure of a land snail, an earthworm, and an insect.

- use modeling clay to sculpt a realistic three-dimensional representation of an animal.

Materials

- land snails, earthworms, and insects—at least 1 each per group of 4 students

- large, well-ventilated containers, 1 for snails and 1 for earthworms

- small containers for insects—clear, ventilated, and covered

- paper plates

- Logsheet 4: Backyard Creatures (page 165)

- hand lenses

- newspapers to cover work areas

- modeling clay

- jumbo paper clips

- thin wire

- scissors

- construction paper rectangles, approximately 4 1/2" x 6"

Getting Ready

1. Before the lesson, enlist your students' help in collecting the following animals:

Earthworms: Obtain earthworms, either from your yard or from a bait shop (see the Yellow Pages for one near you). Keep them refrigerated in a container with some damp earth until ready for use. Feed them cornmeal, coffee grounds, or compost.

Snails: Obtain land snails from your yard or have students bring them from home. Snails are most easily found during fall and spring months. During the day they rest on the underside of leaves or at the base of walls and fences. During the evening or early morning hours, they can be found on lawns. Otherwise, purchase them from a pet shop or a science supply house. Keep snails in a tightly covered, large container with ventilation. Snails are very active at night and will crawl around the classroom if they escape. Sprinkle the snails with water daily. Feed them cornmeal, greens, and bits of eggshell.

Insects: Ask each student to bring an insect to class from a nearby yard or field. Students can bring sow bugs, beetles, butterflies, houseflies, and so on. Tell students to look for sow bugs and beetles under rocks and logs. Houseflies can sometimes be found on windowsills indoors. Point out that students may bring in a dead specimen if it is intact. Have students bring live insects in clear, covered containers with air holes punched through the top.

2. Organize the container of earthworms, the container of snails, small containers of insects, paper plates, logsheets, and hand lenses for easy distribution during the "Observing, Comparing, and Describing" portion of the lesson.

3. Divide the modeling clay into egg-sized lumps. You will need one or more per student. Cut a 6-in. length of wire for each student. Organize the modeling clay, jumbo paper clips, wire segments, scissors, and construction paper rectangles for easy distribution during the "Creating" portion of the lesson.

4. Cover work areas with newspaper.

5. Set aside an area of the classroom where the finished sculptures can be displayed.

note

Students should be organized into groups of four.

Observing, Comparing, and Describing

1. Begin by having students share their knowledge of the various small animals that live in backyards and fields. List their responses on the chalkboard. The following questions are useful in guiding discussion:

What kinds of small animals live in backyards, vacant lots, and fields? *(Worms, snails, mice, beetles, flies, fleas, butterflies, grasshoppers, spiders, etc.)*

Which of these animals are most similar in appearance? *(Animals in the same class or phyla, such as insects, mammals, etc.)*

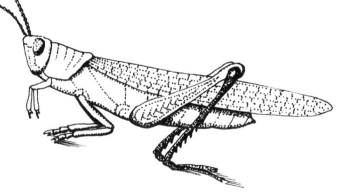

Which of these animals are most different in appearance? *(Answers may vary.)*

In what ways do animals differ in their external structure, or in the arrangement of their body parts? *(In every imaginable way; in having eyes, ears, legs, etc.; in the number of such body parts; etc.)*

What external body parts do all animals have in common? *(None—the animal world is incredibly diverse.)*

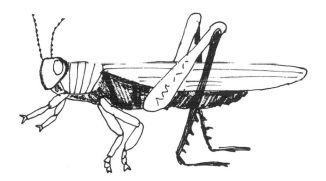

2. Tell students that they will work in groups of four to investigate and compare the external structure of three different animals: a snail, an earthworm, and an insect.

3. Explain that the animals are living creatures and must be handled gently and with respect. Demonstrate how to lift an earthworm carefully by sliding your fingers under it. Demonstrate how to lift a snail by holding its shell and gently pulling upward.

4. Tell students that the earthworms and snails will be on paper plates and should be handled as little as possible. The insects will remain in closed, ventilated containers and must not be handled without permission from the teacher.

note

Some students will not want to touch the animals at all. These students can be encouraged to work with partners who are willing to handle the animals for them while they observe.

5. Distribute hand lenses and copies of Logsheet 4: Backyard Creatures. Tell students that as they each complete the logsheet, they should share ideas and observations with others in the group.

6. Demonstrate the procedure:

Use a hand lens to carefully examine an animal from all sides. Locate those body parts that enable it to eat, move, and breathe. Notice its overall color, size, and shape, and the appearance of each of its parts.

On the logsheet, write a thorough description of the animal. Next to the description, make a quick sketch. Make your sketch larger than life size.

Examine a second, and then a third animal. Record your observations and make a sketch of each animal on the logsheet.

7. When students understand the procedure, ask a member of each group to come forward and collect several animals to take to his or her group. Have these students place two snails and two worms on a paper plate for each group of four students. Students can take as many insects as are available for each group to observe.

Fly
It has six legs and two wings. The head has no neck. Its eyes are large and made of many smaller parts.

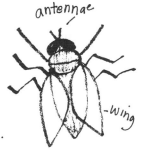

Sowbug
It has two long antennae and two small eyes. It has a thin shell on its back made of sections so it can curl up.

8. As students observe the animals, circulate, and offer assistance as needed.

Drawing Conclusions

Have students share their observations. The following questions are useful in guiding discussion:

What body parts do all three animals have in common? *(Each has a mouth.)*

How do they differ in structure? *(They differ in almost every way.)*

Explaining the Phenomenon

Earthworms, snails, and insects differ greatly from one another in structure. Some of the differences are discussed below.

Earthworms: The smooth body of the earthworm is made up of rings, or segments, called annuli. On each segment, except the first and the last, are four pairs of tiny bristles. These bristles, called *setae,* help the worms move through the earth.

Earthworms have no eyes or ears, but they do have a mouth. They are sensitive to heat, light, and touch. They have no lungs or gills. The worms breathe through their skin, which is in contact with the air found between the small particles of soil. When it rains, these air spaces fill with water, and the worms must come to the surface to breathe, or they die.

Earthworms are *hermaphroditic,* having both male and female reproductive parts. Each worm must mate with another to form eggs. Eggs are laid in a cufflike structure provided by the *clitellum.*

Snails: The snail has no internal skeleton. Inside its shell, it has a small, simple brain, a two-chambered heart, a digestive system, a liver, a lung, kidneys, reproductive organs, and a nervous system.

The land snail has eyes in its two upper tentacles, with which it can detect only light and dark. The lower tentacles contain organs of smell. The snail breathes through a tiny opening, its lung, which is located on the right side of its body near the rim of the shell.

The snail has a long, narrow tongue, the *radula,* which is covered with 27,000 tiny, hooked teeth, arranged in rows. As the snail eats, its tongue moves back and forth like a small saw. The snail's foot secretes mucus to help the snail move over many different kinds of surfaces. Snails are hermaphroditic, containing both male and female reproductive organs. When snails mate, the feet join together.

Insects: There are more than 900,000 described species of insects. Although there are variations in structure among different species, all insects have features in common. The usual insect has three chief divisions in its body: the head, the thorax, and the abdomen.

SAFETY TIP

Remind students to wash their hands thoroughly after handling the animals.

note

There is more information here than should be provided to students in one lesson. Select only the most relevant information to share with students; omit the rest, or leave it for a later session.

insects

*{ head
thorax
abdomen*

The insect's head bears a pair of antennae, a pair of compound eyes and several simple eyes, and a set of mouthparts. The compound eyes are composed of small *ommatidia,* slender cones with light-sensitive receivers at their bases. The mouthparts of insects vary greatly. Mosquitoes have stilettos for piercing skin, flies have a rounded sponging set of mouthparts, and butterflies have a structure that can lap up nectar or coil like a spring when not in use.

The insect's *thorax* contains the body parts used in movement: three pairs of walking legs and, in some insects, two pairs of wings. Insect wings may be leathery, scaly, feathery, and so on. Insect legs have claws, hairs, or suckers to enable the animal to cling to smooth surfaces.

The insect's abdomen contains the reproductive organs. Breathing holes, called *spiracles,* are located along the sides of the abdomen. Adult insects have no lungs, but they pump air in and out through the spiracles. Air is delivered directly to the body tissues.

note

For more information, see "Animals: Background Information" on page 32.

Creating

1. Tell students that one way to observe thoroughly and learn about something is to make a realistic model of it. Explain that they will use modeling clay to make small sculptures of one or more animals.

2. Demonstrate the procedure:

Carefully observe an animal from all sides, including top and bottom.

Shape an egg-sized piece of modeling clay to resemble the overall form of the animal. Make your sculpture larger than life size.

Use your fingers to smooth out any lumps. Shape the clay to resemble the animal on all sides, including the underside.

To add long, thin pieces, for legs, roll bits of clay between your fingers. Attach one end of each length to the body of the sculpture. Smooth away any cracks or lines.

Use the straightened end of a paper clip to add details to the body.

To add antennae, use scissors to cut the 6-in. length of wire into two desired lengths. Curve or straighten the wire to resemble the antennae on the insect. Push the wires into the head.

Place the finished sculpture on a piece of construction paper. Write your name in one corner of the paper.

Make other sculptures as time allows. Add them to the first sculpture on the construction paper.

3. When students understand the procedure, distribute the clay, paper clips, and construction paper, and have them begin. Circulate, and offer assistance as needed.

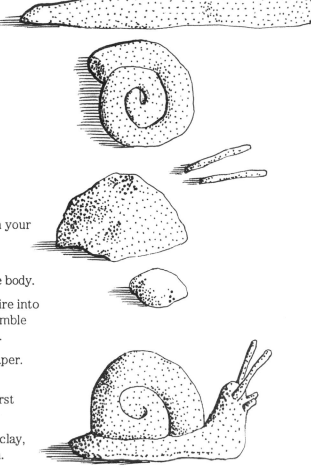

Evaluating

Ask students to look over their finished sculptures and to observe the elements that look most realistic. Have volunteers discuss one thing they especially like about their sculpture and one thing they might do differently next time.

Going Further

Have students generate a list of questions for further investigation. Examples of such questions are:

- *How do different kinds of animals respond to the environment?* Students can investigate the response of various animals to light, touch, sound, and odor. Have students bring to class such animals as snails, earthworms, beetles, and so on. Place an animal in a shoe box with one half covered, so that it is darkened on one side. Have students observe whether the animal goes toward the light or dark side of the box. Tell them to gently touch an animal on its back, head, or side, and observe its reaction to touch. Have students clap hands or make another loud noise near an animal, and observe its reaction to sound. Dip a piece of paper into orange juice or milk. Bring the paper close to the animal's head, without touching the animal, and have students observe the animal's reaction to the smell. Have students record their observations in a journal or logbook.

- *What do different kinds of animals eat?* Have students bring to class such animals as snails, earthworms, beetles, mice, hamsters, and so on. Offer each animal a variety of food, including lettuce leaves, grass, fruit, and seeds. Have students classify animals according to the kinds of foods they eat.

Additional Resources

Goor, Ron, and Goor, Nancy. *Insect Metamorphosis: From Egg to Adult.* New York: Atheneum, 1990.

Kerby, Mona. *Cockroaches.* New York: Watts, 1989.

Overbeck, Cynthia. *Dragonflies.* New York: Lerner, 1982.

Patent, Dorothy. *Spider Magic.* New York: Holiday House, 1982.

● ●

Animals: Background Information

What are animals? The word *animal* comes from the Latin word *anima,* meaning "breath" or "air." Most animals breathe, have a nervous system, eat, and move. Biologists have classified living things into categories called *kingdoms.* Until recently, all organisms were placed into one of two kingdoms: plants, which are green and stationary, and animals, which eat and move about. However, so many living things do not fit into either a plant or an animal category, that other systems were developed. One system used by many biologists includes five kingdoms.

Monera: The simplest of living things; includes bacteria, blue-green algae, and viruses.

Protista: Includes some unicellular algae, protozoa, and some intermediate organisms.

Fungi: Plantlike organisms with cell walls composed largely of chitin.

Plantae: Organisms with cell walls composed of cellulose. Includes red, brown, and green algae, mosses, and the vascular plants (ferns and seed plants).

Animalia: Organisms generally capable of spontaneous movement with cell walls composed of protein. Includes sponges, jellyfish, and worms.

One of the ways animals are classified is by their physical structure. Biologists compare thousands of individual organisms, looking for patterns of similarity. They notice whether the animal is one-celled or composed of many cells. They observe the symmetry of the animal body. They observe and compare both internal and external structures.

The animal kingdom is divided into categories called *phyla,* which are listed below. Phyla are divided into subphyla, classes, and subclasses. A *species* is a group of individuals that have similar structures and the ability to interbreed. They are given a common name, such as robin, or gopher snake.

Phylum Porifera	(sponges)
Phylum Coelenterata	(includes polyps, jellyfishes, corals, and anemones)
Phylum Platyhelminthes	(flatworms)
Phylum Aschelminthes	(roundworms)
Phylum Mollusca	(molluscs—includes snails, clams, and squids)
Phylum Annelida	(segmented worms—includes earthworms)
Phylum Arthropoda	(arthropods—includes spiders, insects, and crustaceans)
Phylum Echinodermaa	(includes sea lilies and starfish)
Phylum Hemichordata	(acorn worms)
Phylum Chordata	(chordates—includes human beings, and all other animals with backbones)

Gyotaku: Fish Printing

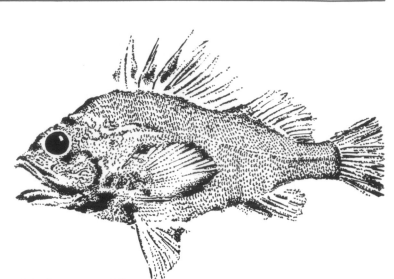

Overview

What is the external structure of a fish? The techniques of *gyotaku,* or fish printing, have been used in Japan for over 100 years. They are used to record catches of fish and to gain ichthyological (fish biology) information. In this activity, students use the techniques of gyotaku to learn about the external structure of fish and to create beautiful prints.

Student Objectives

- identify dorsal fins, caudal fin, anal fin, anus, pelvic fin, pectoral fin, isthmus, nostril, gills, spines, and lateral line on a fish.

- use the gyotaku technique of fish printing.

Materials

- fish, 1 per group of 3 or 4 students

- refrigerator or ice chest with ice

- newspapers to cover work areas

- plastic modeling clay, 1 golf-ball sized lump per group

- straight pins, 6 per group

- black water-base ink (linoleum block ink is best), 1 container per group

- stiff 1/2" brushes, 1 per group

- small watercolor brushes, 1 per group

- newsprint, rice paper, or other absorbent paper

- paper towels

- Logsheet 5: Fish Anatomy (page 166)

Getting Ready

1. Obtain fresh fish from a local market. Select fish with distinct scales, such as perch or rockfish. Wash the fish thoroughly with soap and cold water, and keep them in a refrigerator or an ice chest until ready to use.

2. Cover work areas with newspaper.

3. Arrange printing materials for easy distribution to groups.

note

Students should be organized into groups of four.

4. Draw a rough sketch of an external fish anatomy on the chalkboard, as shown below. Do not label the parts yet.

Observing, Comparing, and Describing

1. Begin by having students share their knowledge of fish anatomy. The following questions are useful in guiding discussion:

What part of its anatomy helps a fish move through the water? *(Fins, tail)*

What part helps it sense its environment? *(Eyes, nostrils, lateral line)*

What part helps it breathe? *(Gills)*

2. Show students the sketch of a generalized external fish anatomy on the chalkboard. Ask students to help you name the parts as you label them. Draw a line to connect each part with its name.

3. Distribute one fish and several paper towels to each group. Have students identify the parts of the fish, using the chalkboard sketch as a guide.

4. Distribute copies of Logsheet 5: Fish Anatomy. Tell students that as they each complete the logsheet, they should share their observations with others in their group.

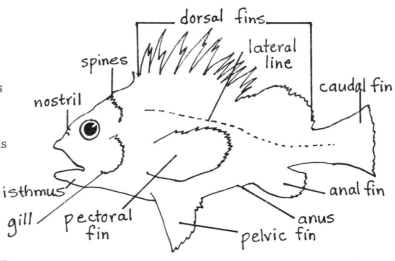

5. When students understand the procedure, have them begin. Circulate, and offer assistance as needed.

Drawing Conclusions

Have students share their descriptions. Ask students to compare different structures on the fish. The following questions are useful in guiding discussion:

What differences did you observe in the appearance of the fins? *(The first dorsal fin has hard, sharp spines, while the other fins have soft, flexible fin rays. Both spines and rays are connected by a thin fleshy material that collects mucus.)*

How did you describe the lateral line? *(As a series of small spots. Some kinds of fish have more than one; the lateral line is a series of small organs the fish uses to sense turbulence and pressure changes.)*

Where did you notice mucus on the body of the fish? *(On the fins, near the anus, gill cover, isthmus, nostrils, and under the pectoral fins; fish secrete mucus to protect themselves from parasites and to help them glide smoothly through the water.)*

Creating

1. Tell students that they will be making *gyotaku* prints of their fish. A successful gyotaku print clearly reveals the anatomical structure of the fish. Gyotaku techniques of fish printing have been used in Japan for over 100 years. Fishers use them to record catches of sport fish. They also help provide ichthyological information to biologists.

2. Demonstrate the procedure:

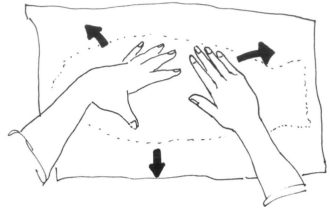

Place a fish on newspaper. Use paper towels to remove as much mucus as possible.

Shape several small lumps of modeling clay into small pancakes approximately 1/2" in diameter. Place a clay pancake under each fin. Spread the fins out over the clay and fix them in position by sticking a pin through the fins into the clay.

Brush on a thin, even coat of ink over the entire fish. Leave the eye blank.

Place a piece of newsprint or rice paper over the fish.

Use your fingers to gently press the paper over the entire surface area of the fish. As you press, move your hand slowly outward from the center of the body. Be careful not to move the paper, or the print will smudge. Remove the paper by lifting one edge and slowly peeling it off the fish.

Use a small brush to paint the eye.

3. When students understand the procedure, distribute clay, pins, ink, brushes, and paper, and have students begin to print their fish. Circulate, and offer assistance as needed.

note
Remind students to wash their hands thoroughly after handling the fish.

Evaluating

After everyone has finished printing, have students compare their prints to the actual fish. The following questions are useful in guiding discussion:

Are all the structures revealed in the print?

Does the print reveal the texture and form of the fish?

Which parts of the print are you most satisfied with?

What might you do differently if you were to make another print?

Going Further

Have students generate a list of questions for further investigation. Examples of such questions are:

■ *On what other kinds of materials can prints be made?* Fish prints can be made on T-shirts or other cloth by using fabric paint. Students can experiment with a wide range of colors. Multiple prints can easily be obtained by thoroughly washing and drying the fish between printings.

■ *What other kinds of natural forms can be used to make gyotaku-type prints?* Gyotaku printing techniques can be used for making prints of such flat-shaped forms as shells, rocks, seaweed, flowers, and other objects. Have students bring in a variety of natural forms and experiment to see which can be used in printmaking.

Additional Resources

Arnosky, J. *Freshwater Fish and Fishing.* New York: Four Winds Press, 1982.

Sattler, Helen. *Sharks, the Super Fish.* New York: Lothrop, 1986.

Muscles, Tendons, Bones, and Joints

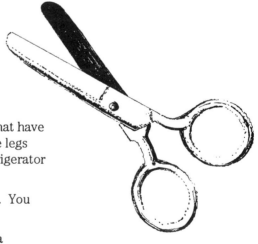

Overview

How do muscles, tendons, bones, and joints contribute to both strength and flexibility in the body? Students dissect a chicken leg to learn about muscle groups and tendons and how they are attached to the bone. They observe the structure and function of the joint. As artists, students then draw a realistic illustration of the human hand, paying close attention to the structure of muscle, tendon, bone, and joint beneath the skin.

Student Objectives

- dissect a chicken leg and observe the structure and function of muscles, tendons, bones, and joints.

- use pencil to draw a realistic illustration of a human hand.

Materials

- chicken legs with drumstick and thigh attached, 1 per student pair

- refrigerator or ice chest with ice

- polystyrene trays, 1 per student pair

- scissors, 1 per student pair

- Logsheet 6: Dissecting a Chicken Leg (page 167), 1 per student pair

- pencils

- hand-wipes

- paper towels

- newspapers to cover work areas

- masking tape in 6" lengths

- white drawing paper, 9" x 12", 2 sheets per student

Getting Ready

1. Obtain chicken legs from a local butcher. You will need legs that have the drumstick and thigh still attached to each other. Wash the legs thoroughly with soap and water. Store them in the school refrigerator or in an ice chest until ready for use.

2. Obtain polystyrene trays from a local butcher or grocery store. You may have students bring clean polystyrene trays from home.

3. For each pair of students, place a chicken leg and scissors on a polystyrene tray. Organize the dissecting materials, logsheets, pencils, hand-wipes, and paper towels for easy distribution during the lesson.

4. Cover work areas with newspaper.

5. Have lengths of masking tape and drawing paper available for distribution during the "Creating" portion of the activity.

Observing, Comparing, and Describing

1. Begin by having students share their knowledge of muscular and skeletal structure. The following questions are useful in guiding discussion:

What is a skeleton? *(The bony, supportive structure of an organism; the framework that protects internal soft tissues and organs in a vertebrate)*

How are the bones in your body held together? *(By ligaments, joints, tendons, and muscles)*

If the bones in your hand were removed, what would your hand be like? *(Soft and flexible, without rigidity)*

What is the purpose, or function, of the skeleton? *(To provide support for internal tissues; to protect internal organs)*

What is a muscle? *(Tissue that functions to produce motion)*

How are the muscles in your body attached to your bones? *(By tendons)*

If the muscles in your hand were removed, what would your hand be like? *(Unable to move, skeletal in appearance)*

2. Tell students that the structure of a chicken leg is similar to the structure of a human arm or leg. Dissecting a chicken leg is a good way to learn about the structure of muscle groups, how they are attached to the bone, and how bones are held together at the joint.

3. Distribute a copy of Logsheet 6: Dissecting a Chicken Leg, to each student pair.

4. Tell students that they will work with a partner to dissect a chicken leg and record their observations on the logsheet. One person may write and sketch while the other dissects, or they may take turns, using the hand-wipes and paper towels to clean and dry their hands.

5. Demonstrate the procedure:

Remove the skin from the chicken leg. Roll it down, much as you might roll down a sock. Observe the external appearance of the leg and record your observations on the logsheet.

Flex the leg. Notice how the different muscles contract and relax. Record your observations.

Cut through the tendons at the base of the leg. Carefully separate the muscle groups. Record your observations.

Cut between the thigh and the lower leg, or drumstick, to expose the joint. Work carefully to locate all of the parts. Record your observations.

note

Students should be organized into pairs for the "Observing, Comparing, and Describing" portion of this activity.

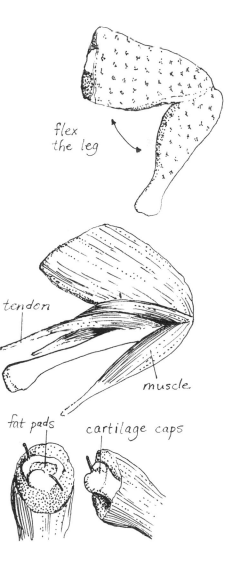

flex the leg

tendon

muscle

fat pads   cartilage caps

SAFETY TIP
Caution students not to put their hands in their mouths when handling the raw poultry.

6. When students understand the procedure, distribute to each pair a polystyrene tray, pair of scissors, chicken leg, and several hand-wipes and paper towels. Have them begin. Circulate, and offer assistance as needed.

Drawing Conclusions

Have students share their observations. The following questions are useful in guiding discussion:

What did you observe under the skin? *(Feather bumps, underlayer of fat, thin connective tissue, capillaries)*

What happened when you flexed the leg? *(Opposite pairs of muscles moved differently—one contracted as the other relaxed.)*

What are examples of similar muscle movement in your own bodies? *(Relaxation and contraction of muscle pairs in thighs, lower legs, upper arms, lower arms, fingers, toes, etc.)*

What did you observe when you cut the tendons and examined the muscles in the leg? *(Each muscle group was encased in a thin sheath; large blood vessels were visible.)*

How would you describe the joint? *(Like a hinge, with a cap of cartilage and fatty tissue around it; the cartilage cap looks like a piece of white plastic, and the fatty tissue is yellow.)*

Explaining the Phenomenon

Your *skeleton* is the framework that supports you—it holds you up and provides protection to your internal organs. When you were born, you had 300 bones, as all human babies do. By the time you reach adulthood, you will have 206 bones in your body, because some will have fused together.

Joints enable your bones to move together. You can bend, stretch, pivot, and swivel because of your joints. Your body has several kinds of joints, each capable of a different sort of movement. For instance, your elbow has a joint like a hinge, while your ankle has structure more like a ball and socket. Joints contain smooth white cartilage and fatty deposits to reduce the friction that results when two bones move against each other.

Muscles are tissues that produce movement in the body. Your body is able to sit, stand, walk, and run because of just one muscle action—contraction. Muscles can contract and make themselves shorter, or they can relax. When you flex your biceps, you can feel the muscle contract. It pulls together into a kind of heap. Feel the muscle beneath your arm, opposite the biceps, as you straighten out your arm. You will notice that it contracts as the biceps relax. All of your muscles work in teams, one opposite the other. As one contracts, the other relaxes.

Tendons are tough bands of white tissue that connect muscle to bone. Tendons are made of a very strong, fibrous material. They are so strong that bones will usually break before tendons will tear. Your tendons give you flexibility. If your tendons flex easily, you can bend over and touch

Note

Have students use the hand-wipes and paper towels to thoroughly clean and dry the scissors when they are finished. You may want to retrieve the dissected chicken legs if you have a cat at home (the meat can be cooked and removed from the bone). The polystyrene trays can be washed thoroughly for future use as dissecting trays.

SAFETY TIP

Be sure to have students thoroughly wash their hands with soap and water after they have finished dissecting.

your toes. If your tendons have not been stretched for a while and
have lost some of their flexibility, it can be difficult to even bend over.

Creating

1. Tell students that artists have always been interested in human
   anatomy, the study of the structure of the human body. By
   learning about anatomy, artists are better able to draw the
   human body realistically.

2. Tell students that they will be applying their knowledge of
   muscles, tendons, joints, and bones as they draw a realistic
   illustration of their hand.

3. Have students carefully observe one of their hands. The
   following questions are useful in guiding observation:

   What do you notice about the back of your hand as you wiggle
   your fingers? *(The tendons move over the knuckles and slide
   over the back of the hand.)*

   Where is the structure of the bones and joints visible beneath
   the skin? *(In the knuckles and at the wrist)*

   What do you notice about the appearance of your skin on the
   back of your hand? *(Creases over joints, smooth over muscle
   and bone)*

4. Explain that drawing a realistic picture of
   something requires very careful observation.
   Demonstrate the procedure:

   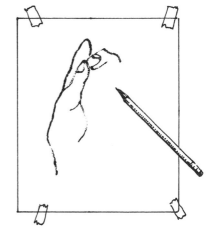

   Place two sheets of drawing paper on the
   table or desk in front of you, several inches
   apart, as shown.

   Place your "model" hand on one sheet of
   paper in an interesting pose. You will draw
   the model on the other sheet.

   When you are in a comfortable position, tape
   both sheets of paper to the table so that they
   won't move around as you are drawing.

   Carefully observe the overall shape of your
   hand. Notice the lines of the finger bones,
   the slight curves of the muscles and tendons,
   and the bulges at the knuckles and joints.

   Begin to draw. First, sketch the overall shape of your hand.
   Proceed from edge to edge. As you draw, notice the proportions
   of your hand. For example, notice how long your fingers are in
   relation to the width of your hand.

   Draw slowly and take your time. Do not panic if a line comes out
   "wrong"—it can be corrected.

After you have drawn the overall shape of your hand, begin to draw
the faint lines and creases you observe in your skin. Add the
fingernails, and such details as small hairs or veins.

5. When students understand the procedure, distribute the drawing
paper and have them begin. Circulate, and offer assistance as
needed.

Evaluating

Ask students to look over their finished drawings and notice the
elements that look most realistic. Have volunteers discuss one thing
they especially like about their drawing, and one thing they might do
differently next time.

Going Further

Have students generate a list of questions for further investigation.
Examples of such questions are:

- *What are bones made of?* Students can investigate the structure
and composition of bones by dissecting a soup bone. Obtain several
soup bones from your local butcher. Ask the butcher to cut a
cylindrical bone such as the shin lengthwise so that your students can
observe the inside.

  Have students hold the halves of the bone together and notice the
appearance of the end of the bone. They will see an external layer of
calcified bone covering a layer of spongy bone, which in turn covers
the marrow. Have students examine some of the marrow under a
microscope to observe blood cells. Have students pull away the
periosteum, the outer skin of the bone. On a fresh bone, they will
observe small red dots where blood vessels enter the bone.

- *Do stretching exercises increase the flexibility of the tendons?*
Students can investigate the influence of regular stretching exercises
on the flexibility of their own bodies. They can take baseline
measurements of the following body parts:

  Spine: How close can the head come to the toes when the student
arches back from a horizontal position on his or her stomach?

  Hip: How close can a straight leg come to the nose when when the
student raises it from a horizontal position on his or her back?

  Thighs: How close can the back come to the floor when a student is
on his or her knees and leans back with the body in a straight
position?

  After taking baseline measurements, students can begin a program of
regular stretching exercise in which they repeat and gradually extend
the positions described above. They can take periodic measurements
and record their findings in a journal or logbook.

SAFETY TIP

Caution students to move their
bodies carefully and slowly while
doing stretching exercises. Students
should never force themselves to
stretch beyond their comfort level.

Additional Resources

Bruun, Ruth Dowling, & Bertel Brunn. *The Human Body.* New York: Random House, 1982.

Edwards, Betty. *Drawing on the Artist Within.* New York: Simon & Schuster, 1986.

Showers, Paul. *You Can't Make a Move Without Your Muscles.* New York: Crowell, 1982.

Stein, Sara. *The Body Book.* New York: Workman, 1992.

Roots and Shoots

Overview

What variations can we observe in the external structure of vascular plants? How do their roots, stems, and leaves differ? In this activity, students examine a variety of plants and compare their external characteristics. As artists, they apply their knowledge of plant structure in constructing a collage that illustrates the wonderful variety of plant forms.

Student Objectives

- observe variation in the external structure of roots, stems, and leaves of different plant species.

- create a collage using different materials, shapes, and textures to create a variety of plant forms.

Materials

- plants with roots attached, such as weeds and grasses—3 different plants per group of 4 students

- hand lenses

- Logsheet 7: Plant Structure (page 168)

- pencils

- construction paper, 18" x 24", 1 blue sheet per student, 1 brown sheet per student pair, and 1 of each color for the teacher

- collage materials, such as scraps of tissue paper, wallpaper, wrapping paper, fabric, construction paper, lengths of yarn, ribbon, string, and bits of aluminum foil

- paste

- cotton swabs, craft sticks, or other small items for applying paste

- large shallow containers to hold collage materials—1 per group of 4 students

- scissors

- newspapers to cover work areas

Getting Ready

1. Collect a variety of plant specimens for students to examine. If the weather permits, take students outdoors just prior to the activity and have them collect various weeds and grasses. Make sure students include the roots with each sample. Plants can be carefully dug up from the soil with trowels or old stainless steel forks and placed into plastic bags.

Plant specimens can also be obtained from a local nursery. A square foot of grass sod can be broken up into enough pieces for an entire class; small vegetables can also be carefully removed from their potting soil and examined.

Still another way to collect a variety of plant specimens is to have students plant such seeds as carrot, radish, bean, grass, and marigold several weeks prior to the activity.

2. For each group of four students, organize four different plants, four hand lenses, pencils, and logsheets for distribution during the "Observing, Comparing, and Describing" portion of the lesson.

3. For each group, place an assortment of collage materials into a shoe box or other shallow container. Organize paste, cotton swabs, collage materials, scissors, and colored construction paper for distribution during the "Creating" portion of the lesson.

4. Cover work areas with newspaper.

Observing, Comparing, and Describing

1. Begin by having students share their knowledge of plants. The following questions are useful in guiding discussion:

What is a plant? *(An organism whose cells are covered with cellulose walls; a member of the plant kingdom)*

What is an example of an extremely small plant? *(Algae)*

What is an example of an extremely large plant? *(Redwood or sequoia tree)*

What are some plant parts? *(Roots, stems, leaves, flowers, etc.)*

What are some plants that are missing some of these plant parts? *(Algae)*

2. Explain that the plants with which we are most familiar are the *vascular plants.* They are given this name because they have a system of vessels in their roots, stems, and leaves that carries water throughout the plant. Examples of vascular plants include ferns, conifers, flowers, grasses, and cacti.

3. Tell students that they will be working in groups of four to compare the structure of three kinds of vascular plants.

4. Distribute copies of Logsheet 7: Plant Structure. Tell students that as they each complete the logsheet, they should share observations with others in the group.

5. Demonstrate the procedure:

Carefully examine each plant's roots with a hand lens. Notice similarities and differences. Does one root appear larger, with smaller roots branching from it? Or are all the roots the same size? Can you see root hairs?

Note
Students should be organized into groups of four.

Write a description of each plant's roots on the logsheet.

Carefully examine each plant's stems. Notice similarities and differences. What is their color? What is their texture—smooth, rough, or fuzzy? What is their shape—round, flat, or ovular?

Write a description of each plant's stems on the logsheet.

Carefully examine each plant's leaves. Notice similarities and differences. How are they arranged on the stem—opposite each other, or alternately arranged? What is their color? What is their texture and shape?

Write a description of each plant's leaves on the logsheet.

Next to the descriptions, draw a quick sketch of each plant.

6. When students understand the procedure, distribute the plants and have them begin. Circulate, and offer assistance as needed.

Plant #1
The root is long with smaller roots coming out from the sides. The stem has branches and it is round and prickly. The leaves are long, bumpy and prickly.

Plant #2
The grass has small branching roots. The stem is smooth and ends in a leaf. The leaves are long and narrow and rough. They wrap around the stem.

Drawing Conclusions

Have students share their observations. The following questions are useful in guiding discussion:

What similarities did you observe among the plants' roots? What differences?

What similarities did you observe among the plants' stems? What differences?

What similarities did you observe among the plants' leaves? What differences?

Explaining the Phenomenon

The number of different plants that inhabit our world is enormous. We do not even know how many there are, because there are still unknown plants that have not yet been identified. The number of plants that have been identified is impressive. There are nearly 3,000 recorded species in the carrot family, and about 4,500 species of grass.

One of the ways plants are classified is by their physical structure. *Botanists,* scientists who study plants, compare various kinds of plants to decide whether they are of the same or of a different species. They examine the roots, stems, leaves, flower parts, and so on. A *species* is a group of individuals that have similar structures and the ability to interbreed. They are given a common name, such as dandelion, or rose.

Note

For more information about plant classification, see "Plants: Background Information" on page 48.

Creating

1. Tell students that when an artist illustrates an object in as many different forms as possible, he or she creates a design called a *variation on a theme*. Explain that they will use variation on a theme to create collage pictures of plants. *Collage* is artwork made by gluing bits of paper, fabric, scraps, photographs, or other materials to a flat surface.

2. Demonstrate the procedure:

Draw a gently sloping horizontal line across the lower third of a sheet of brown paper. Cut along the sloping line. Paste the smaller of the brown pieces to the bottom of the blue construction paper. The brown area will represent the soil, and the blue area will represent the sky.

Let your partner cut a similar piece from the remaining brown paper and paste it to his or her blue paper.

Use pencil to sketch plants, drawing the roots below the soil line and the stems, leaves, and flowers above. Make each plant different in some way. Fill the entire paper with your design.

Cut out leaf and flower shapes from the collage materials. Lay them on top of your design to see how they look.

Cut out yarn, string, or strips of paper to serve as roots or stems. Arrange them on the paper until you have a design you like.

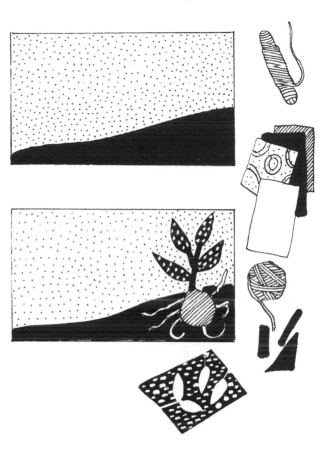

Use a cotton swab or craft stick to apply paste to the design. Paste the leaves, flowers, roots, and stems to the paper.

Finally, add insects or birds or other elements if you wish.

3. When students understand the procedure, distribute the materials, and have them begin. Circulate, and offer assistance as needed.

Note

Remind students that, as artists, they can be creative. Rather than drawing realistic-looking plants, they may want to add such imaginary features as pizza flowers, tennis-shoe leaves, and so on.

Evaluating

Display the finished collages for everyone to see. Have students compare the variety of forms and materials used by their classmates.

Going Further

Have students generate a list of questions for further investigation. Examples of such questions are:

- *How do seeds differ in structure?* Students can examine and compare both the external and internal structures of various kinds of seeds. Soak a collection of seeds overnight, and have students dissect them by cutting them crosswise with scissors. Students will observe two main classes of seeds: those that divide into two parts are called dicotyledons (such as beans, peas, and peanuts), and those that do not divide are called *monocotyledons* (such as corn and oats). Have students record their observations in a journal or logbook.

- *How do trees differ in structure?* Take the class on a walking field trip through local neighborhoods and have them notice the variation in the size and shape of trees. Students can compare the arrangement of branches on the trunk, the texture of the trunk, the arrangement of leaves on stems, or the shape of the leaves. Students can record their observations on a chart with tally marks, as shown.

triangle

oval

rectangle

Comparing the External Structure of Trees					
Shape				Support	
triangle	oval	rectangle	other	branching	single

Additional Resources

Hamer, Martyn. *Trees.* New York: Watts, 1983.

Lerner, Carol. *Plant Families.* New York: Morrow, 1989.

Lowery, Larry. "Plants," in *The Everyday Science Sourcebook.* Palo Alto, Calif.: Dale Seymour, 1985.

Wilson, Ron. *How Plants Grow.* New York: Larousse, 1980.

Plants: Background Information

A *taxonomist* is a scientist who classifies organisms. Linnaeus (1707–1778) is often called the father of classification for having established a system of naming an organism by giving its genus and species. The genus name comes first and always starts with a capital letter. The species name comes second. Both words are italicized and are in Latin. Thus, the common dandelion is named *Taraxacum officinale.*

A group of species that are so similar they are thought to be related are placed in a *genus.* A genus is placed in a *family,* which is placed in an *order,* which is placed in a *class,* which is placed in a *division* or *phylum,* which is placed into a *kingdom.* The plant kingdom is commonly divided into the following five phyla.

Phylum Rhodophyta	(Red Algae)
Phylum Phaeophyta	(Brown Algae)
Phylum Chlorophyta	(Green Algae)
Phylum Bryophyta	(Mosses)
Phylum Tracheophyta	(Vascular Plants)

Flowers

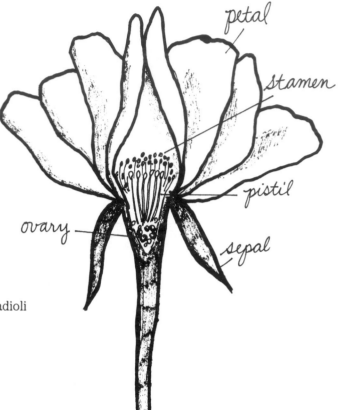

Overview

What is the structure of a flower? In this activity, students identify the various parts of a flower. Next, they dissect the flower to reveal its reproductive structure. Using the drawing techniques of looking, studying, eye-hand coordination, and shading, students then illustrate the flower and label its parts.

Student Objectives

- describe and sketch the parts of a flower: sepals, petals, stamens, anthers, filaments, pistil, stigma, style, ovary, and ovules.

- use drawing techniques of looking, studying, eye-hand coordination, and shading.

Materials

- complete flowers such as tulips, daffodils, roses, or gladioli

- newspapers to cover work areas

- hand lenses

- scissors

- Logsheet 8: Flower Structure (page 169)

- drawing paper, 9" x 12"

- pencils

- tape

Getting Ready

1. Obtain flowers from a garden or a local nursery. One potted azalea plant will yield enough blooms for an entire class. If you plan to have students bring flowers from home, be sure to specify the flowers you want, such as roses or iris. Otherwise, you run the risk of having 25 different flower types to dissect, many of which will be unfamiliar to you.

2. Draw a diagram of a generalized flower on the board, as shown. Label the floral parts.

3. Organize flowers, hand lenses, scissors, pencils, and logsheets for easy distribution during the activity.

4. Cover work areas with newspaper.

Note

Students should be organized into groups of four.

Observing, Comparing, and Describing

1. Begin by having students share their knowledge of
flowers. The following questions are useful in guiding
discussion:

What is your favorite flower? *(Answers will
vary.)*

How are all flowers similar? *(They contain
structures capable of spore production.)*

How do various flowers differ? *(By number, size,
color, and shape of such floral structures as
petals, stamen, sepals, and pistils; by having
petals attached above or below the ovary; by
arrangement of petals and sepals)*

How large or small can flowers be? *(Larger than
a human hand, as a magnolia, or microscopically small, as
the blooms of a floating Wolffia)*

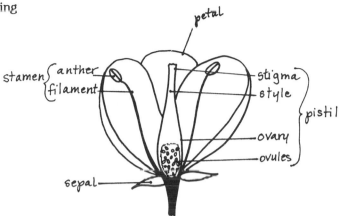

2. Have students attempt to visualize a flower they are familiar
with. Ask, "How many petals does it have? What does the
center of the bloom look like?" Point out that although we see
flowers everywhere, we usually know very little about their
structure.

3. Draw students' attention to the diagram of a generalized flower
on the chalkboard. Identify the floral parts: sepals, petals,
stamens, anthers, filaments, pistil, stigma, style, ovules, and
ovary.

4. Distribute copies of Logsheet 8: Flower Structure. Tell students
that they will work in groups to observe a flower and describe its
parts. Tell students that as they each complete the logsheet,
they should share ideas and observations with others in the
group.

5. Demonstrate how to describe and draw a quick sketch of each
flower part on the logsheet.

6. Distribute the same kind of flower to every student. Ask
students to observe the flower carefully and to work with others
in their groups to identify the floral parts. Circulate, and offer
assistance as needed.

Drawing Conclusions

1. Have a member of each group share descriptions of one or more
floral parts. (Descriptions will vary, depending on the kind of
flower used.)

2. Ask students to notice similarities and differences between the
diagram of the generalized flower and the actual flower they
observed.

Note

For more information, see "Flowers:
Background Information" on page 53.

Creating

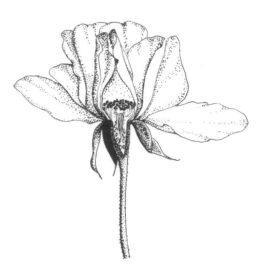

1. Tell students that one way to observe and learn about something is to draw it.

2. Demonstrate how to dissect a flower:

Use your fingers to remove the sepals on one side of a flower.

Next, carefully remove the petals, as shown. Have students notice whether or not the stamens are attached to the base of the petals; this fact is used in identification of flowers.

Use scissors to cut a cross section of a flower. Be sure to cut through the ovary so that the compartments holding the ovules are exposed. Point out that these compartments will be either in groups of three or five.

3. When students understand the procedure, distribute the scissors and have them dissect their flowers. Circulate, and offer assistance as needed.

4. Tell students that they will use pencil to draw the flower larger than life size. Explain that they should try to draw exactly what they see. This kind of careful drawing, based on observation, is called *illustration.*

5. Explain that drawing a realistic picture of something requires very careful looking. Demonstrate the procedure:

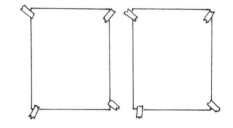

Place two sheets of drawing paper on the table or desk in front of you, several inches apart, as shown.

When you are in a comfortable position, tape both sheets of paper to the table so that they won't move around as you are drawing.

Place your dissected flower on one sheet of paper so that the internal parts are visible. You will draw the flower on the other sheet.

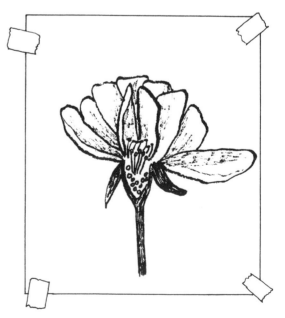

Carefully observe the overall shape of the flower. Notice the lines of the stem, the slight curves of sepals and petals, and so on.

Begin to draw. First, sketch the overall shape of the flower. Draw it larger than life, so that it fills the page. Proceed from edge to edge. As you draw, notice the proportions of the flower. For example, notice how long the petals are in relation to the stamens.

Draw slowly and take your time. Do not panic if a line comes out "wrong"—it can be corrected.

6. When students understand the procedure, distribute the drawing paper, pencils, and tape. Circulate, and offer assistance as needed. Remind students to draw the flower larger than life.

7. When students have completed their drawings, demonstrate the technique of shading. Move a pencil back and forth lightly to shade a small area. Tell students that they should use their pencil tips in a similar way to fill in darker colored areas of the flower with light shading.

Evaluating

Have students evaluate their finished illustrations. The following questions are useful in guiding discussion:

What part or parts of your drawing are you most pleased with?

Does the shading look even?

Are the lines distinct and clear?

Is there anything you would do differently if you were to make another drawing?

Going Further

Have students generate a list of questions for further investigation. Examples of such questions are:

- *What other variations in flower structure can be observed?* Students can dissect and illustrate several kinds of flowers and compare similarities and differences in their structure. Have them record their observations in a journal or logbook.

- *What do flower parts look like under magnification?* Students can use microscopes to take a closer look at the structure of flower parts. Anthers may be examined under a hand lens and then dissected to show the pollen chambers. Students can examine a prepared slide of pollen grains. The different shapes of pollen grains from different plants can be compared.

Additional Resources

Kirkpatrick, Rena K. *Look at Flowers*. Milwaukee: Raintree, 1985.

Robbins, Ken. *A Flower Grows*. New York: Dial, 1990.

Selsam, Millicent. *Tree Flowers*. New York: Morrow, 1986.

Stein, Sara. *The Science Book*. New York: Workman, 1979.

• •

Flowers: Background Information

Flowering plants are the most recent plants on earth. They are also the most complex. No fossil remains of the first flowers have been found, so the transition forms that led to modern flowers are not known. Once developed, flowering plants came to dominate the land, and they are now the most conspicuous plants on earth.

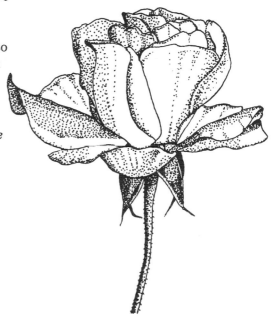

The flower is a specialized organ for plant reproduction. *Complete flowers* have sepals, petals, stamens, and pistils. *Incomplete flowers* lack one or more of these parts. For instance, in the sycamore, willow, alder, grasses, and sedges, sepals and petals are missing or reduced to hairs or scales.

Flowers vary in one or more details, and every imaginable possibility can be found in nature. Sepals may be large or small, green and leaflike, as on a rose, or brightly colored and petal-like,

as on a fuchsia. Petals may be attached below the ovary or above it.
Petals may be separate, as on a daisy, or fused into a single tube, as on a
honeysuckle. Reproductive parts also vary. An *imperfect flower* lacks
either pistils or stamens.

Interactions

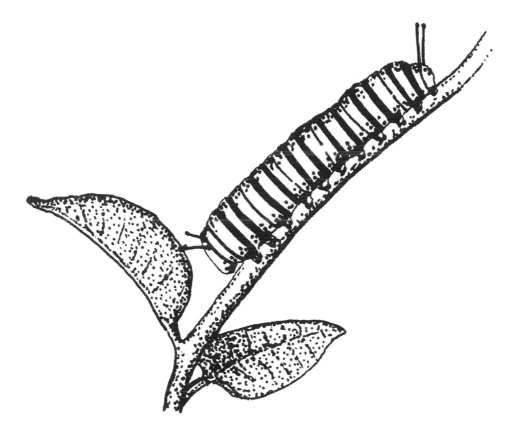

The Theme of Interactions

The investigations in this section are organized around the theme of interactions. *Interactions* are defined as "mutual or reciprocal actions or influences." By exploring interactions within the disciplines of biology, geology, and physics, students learn about the many different kinds of interactions in systems.

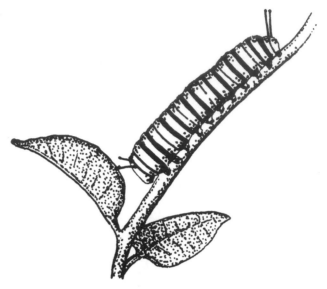

Students learn about physical and chemical interactions between atoms and molecules by observing such phenomena as the formation of crystals, the reaction of gypsum (plaster of Paris) with water, the capillary action of water in various kinds of papers, and the neutralization of acids and bases. By observing and comparing the characteristics of different plant and animal species, they learn how each species has adapted to better fit its environment.

As artists, students learn to experiment with the interactions of different elements of design. They explore the interactions of positive and negative shapes in drawing, painting, and sculpture and investigate the way that dark and light colors can be used to create a sense of contrast in a work of art. Students also learn to experiment with the interactions of different art media, such as art chalk and tempera paint, and watercolor and wax.

Interactions: Color Combinations

Overview

How do primary colors interact to create secondary and tertiary colors? In this activity, students use watercolors to discover how many ways two or more colors can be combined to create new colors. They then create color wheels, arrangements of colors that show the relationships among the various colors and hues.

Student Objectives

- experiment to discover the combinations of colors that create secondary and tertiary colors.

- use color-mixing techniques with watercolors to create a color wheel.

Materials

- watercolor sets, 1 per student

- brushes

- containers to hold water, such as cut-off milk cartons or plastic cups

- paper towels, 2–3 per student

- Logsheet 9: Color Mixing (page 170)

- wax crayons, white

- Logsheet 10: The Color Wheel (page 171)

- newspapers to cover work areas

Getting Ready

1. Organize the watercolor sets, brushes, containers of water, paper towels, wax crayons, and logsheets for easy distribution during the lesson.

2. Cover work areas with newspaper.

3. Set aside an area of the classroom where the color wheels can be laid flat to dry.

note

Students should be organized into groups of four.

Observing, Comparing, and Describing

1. Begin by having students share their knowledge of color. The following questions are useful in guiding discussion:

What different colors can you name? *(Red, blue, yellow, green, orange, purple, magenta, turquoise, etc.)*

If you had just three colors of paint: red, blue, and yellow—how many other colors could you make? *(All the colors of the spectrum plus such colors as black, gray, and brown.)*

How many shades of blue are in this room? *(Answers will vary.)*

Why can we see colors in light but not in total darkness? *(Without light, we cannot see; we see colors because of the way light reflects to our eyes from different surfaces.)*

2. Explain that *color* is a phenomenon of light. As light in the classroom strikes the objects around us, some of that light *reflects,* or bounces back, to our eyes. Some surfaces reflect light we perceive as red, while others reflect light we perceive as blue, or green, and so on.

3. Tell students that they will work in groups of four to investigate the interaction of different-colored paints. Explain that an *interaction* occurs when two or more things influence or change each other in some way. For example, when two colors of paint are combined, their pigments interact to reflect a new, different color.

4. Distribute copies of Logsheet 9: Color Mixing. Tell students that as they each complete the logsheet, they should share ideas and observations with others in the group.

5. Show students a watercolor set. Explain that they will be using only three colors during the investigation: red, blue, and yellow.

6. Demonstrate the procedure:

First, dip your brush in water, and then wipe it against the edge of the container to remove excess water.

Move the bristles back and forth against a color pan to load paint onto the brush.

Dab color onto the paint tray (the inside of the lid of the watercolor set).

Rinse the brush, and then add a second color to the first on the tray.

Experiment by adding different amounts of color until you obtain the color you want.

On the logsheet, list the colors you mixed together to create the desired color. Paint a sample area on the logsheet next to the list.

Wipe the paint tray periodically with a paper towel so that you will always have a clean surface on which to mix colors.

7. When students understand the procedure, distribute the materials and have them begin. Circulate, and offer assistance as needed.

Drawing Conclusions

Have a member from each group share the group's results. The following questions are useful in guiding discussion:

What colors are impossible to create by mixing? *(Red, blue, and yellow—the primary colors)*

What colors are obtained by mixing red, blue, and yellow? *(Mixing pairs creates orange, green, and purple, the secondary colors; mixing all three creates black or dark brown.)*

How many ways can black be obtained? (By mixing all primary colors, all secondary colors, or pairs of such complementary colors as blue and orange, red and green, or yellow and purple)

What did your group find most surprising when you mixed various colors? *(Probably that some shades of purple, green, or orange are impossible to obtain, because each color pigment is somewhat impure.)*

Explaining the Phenomenon

Visible light is made up of the colors of the rainbow: red, orange, yellow, green, blue, indigo, and violet. This rainbow spread of colors is called the *spectrum*.

When light strikes a brush stroke of yellow paint, all of the colors of the rainbow shine on it, but yellow is the only color we see. This is because the yellow wavelengths of light are reflected from the paint back to our eyes, where color receptors in our eyes send a message of yellow to the brain. The other wavelengths are mostly absorbed by the paint.

Red, blue, and yellow are called *primary colors* because these colors are the basis for mixing all other colors. Such colors as orange, green, and purple are called *secondary colors* because they are created by mixing pairs of primary colors. When three or more different colors are combined, they create *tertiary colors*.

When an artist combines two colors of paint, such as blue and yellow, the particles of the two pigments interact to form a mixture. The green color the artist sees is a mixture of the frequencies of visible light reflected by the blue and yellow paint particles.

note

For more information about light, see "Light: Background Information" on page 152.

Creating

1. Tell students that the relationships between primary and secondary colors can easily be seen on a color wheel.

2. Distribute copies of Logsheet 10: The Color Wheel. Explain that they will use mixing techniques with watercolors to color the wheel.

3. Demonstrate the procedure:

First, trace over the lines on the color wheel with a white wax crayon. Press hard as you draw. The wax lines will keep the different colors clearly separate.

Next, paint the "yellow" area of the color wheel.

Dab yellow watercolor onto the paint tray (the inside lid of the watercolor set). Rinse the brush, and then add a small amount of red to mix an orange-yellow. Paint the "orange-yellow" area of the wheel.

Mix equal amounts of red and yellow to create orange. Place the orange next to the orange-yellow.

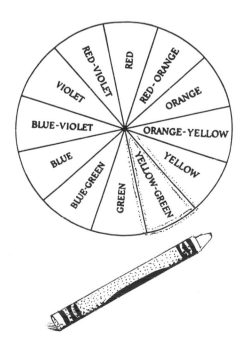

Mix a large amount of red and a small amount of yellow to create red-orange. Paint the red-orange in the area next to the red.

Continue mixing colors and adding them to the wheel until the entire wheel has been filled.

4. When students understand the procedure, distribute the color wheel logsheets and have them begin. Circulate, and offer assistance as needed.

Evaluating

1. Display the finished color wheels for everyone to see. Have students identify pairs of colors that lie opposite each other on the wheel. Tell students that these color pairs are called *complementary colors*.

2. Point out the slight changes in color that lie between each primary color. These changes, or gradations in color, are called *hues*. Ask students to find examples in the color wheels where neighboring hues are clearly distinct from each other.

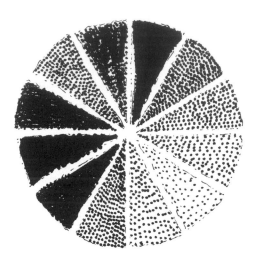

Going Further

Have students generate a list of questions for further investigation. Examples of such questions are:

- *Do colored lights combine to create new colors as do paint pigments?* The following demonstration illustrates the difference between combinations of colored lights and combinations of colored pigments. Obtain three flashlights of the same size that produce about the same amount of light. Cover the front of one with layers of red cellophane, one with dark blue cellophane, and one with green cellophane. Experiment with the number of layers needed for each flashlight until all three produce colored light of equal intensity. Next, shine all three flashlights at one spot on a white surface. The spot will appear white.

  Students will notice that combining various colors of light produces white, whereas combining the same colors of paint pigment produces black. When primary colored lights are combined, they add to each other, so that all the color wavelengths are reflected, producing white. When pigments are combined, they subtract from each other, so that all the color wavelengths are absorbed, producing black.

- *Why is the sky blue?* Here's a classroom demonstration that simulates blue skies and sunset. Set a large, clear pitcher of water on a table where everyone can see it. Darken the room. Position a flashlight next to the pitcher so that its beam penetrates the water. Students will notice little change in the color of the beam. Add a few drops of milk to the water, and the beam of light will turn orange. The molecules of milk scatter the blue light in all directions before it can reach your eyes, just as the atmosphere's molecules do for the rays of sunlight at sunset. Have students look through the side of the pitcher, perpendicular to the beam. They will see blue light, scattered in all directions, just as the atmosphere scatters blue light from sunlight to give us blue skies.

Additional Resources

Lowery, Larry. "Light," in *The Everyday Science Sourcebook*. Palo Alto, Calif.: Dale Seymour, 1985.

Strongin, Herb. "Looking at Light" in *Science on a Shoestring*. Menlo Park, Calif.: Addison-Wesley, 1991.

Water Interactions

Overview

How do two water drops interact? How does water interact with such other substances as construction paper, newspaper, aluminum foil, and wax? Students experiment to compare the interaction of water drops with other materials. Then, as artists, they use the interaction of water and wax to create a crayon-resist painting with watercolors.

Student Objectives

- observe and compare the interaction of water with itself and such other substances as construction paper, newspaper, aluminum foil, and wax.

- use wax and watercolor to create a crayon-resist painting.

Materials

- small containers, such as cut-off milk cartons or plastic or paper cups, 1 per 2 students

- food coloring: blue, green, or red

- drinking straws

- small squares of construction paper, newspaper, aluminum foil, and wax paper, approximately 4" x 4", 2 each per group of 4 students

- Logsheet 11: Water Interactions (page 172)

- pencils

- white construction paper, 9" x 12"

- watercolors

- brushes

- water containers, such as cut-off milk cartons and coffee cans

- newspapers to cover work areas

- wax crayons, light-colored

- (optional) cooking oil

Getting Ready

1. For each group of four students, provide one container 1/2 full of colored water. (Use a few drops of food coloring to color the water.) Place four straws in each container.

2. Organize small squares of construction paper, newspaper, aluminum foil, wax paper, and logsheets for easy distribution during the "Observing, Comparing, and Describing" portion of the lesson.

3. Organize pencils, sheets of construction paper, crayons, watercolors, brushes, and additional containers of water for easy distribution during the "Creating" portion of the lesson.

4. Cover work areas with newspaper.

5. Set aside an area of the classroom where finished paintings can be laid flat to dry.

Observing, Comparing, and Describing

1. Begin by having students share their knowledge of water. The following questions are useful in guiding discussion:

How is water similar to other liquids? *(It flows; it can change its state from a liquid to a solid or a gas, etc.)*

How is water different from other liquids? *(It is composed of two hydrogen atoms and one oxygen atom; it has different properties.)*

To what substances does water cling? *(Substances that attract its molecules, such as wood, glass, various papers, etc.)*

What substances repel, or push away, water? *(Substances that repel its molecules, such as oil, wax, etc.)*

2. Tell students that they will work in groups of four to investigate the interaction of water with several substances: construction paper, newspaper, aluminum foil, and wax. Write the names of these substances on the chalkboard.

3. Distribute copies of Logsheet 11: Water Interactions. Tell students that as they each complete the logsheet, they should share ideas and observations with others in the group.

4. Demonstrate the procedure:

Place pieces of four different materials on the desk or table in front of you: construction paper, newspaper, aluminum foil, and wax paper.

Fold over the top third of a straw, and pinch the double portion of the straw (not the fold).

Squeeze the straw as you dip it into the water. Stop squeezing, and then lift the straw out of the water.

Squeeze a drop of water onto one of the materials.

note
Students should be organized into groups of four.

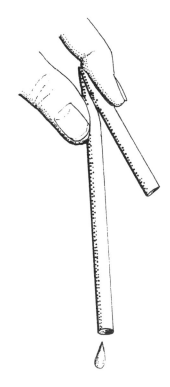

Observe the drop from the top and side. Write a description of the drop on the logsheet. Next to the description, draw a quick, larger than life-size sketch showing both top and side views.

Place a water drop on each of the remaining materials. Describe and sketch the appearance of each drop.

To observe the interaction of two or more water drops, first place a water drop on a square of wax paper. Nearby, place a second water drop. Using a straw, gently push the first water drop toward the second drop and observe what happens. How close can the two drops come before they join to form a single drop? Experiment with several drops. Record your observations on the logsheet.

5. When students understand the procedure, distribute the materials, and have them begin. Circulate, and offer assistance as needed.

Drawing Conclusions

Have students share their observations. The following questions are useful in guiding discussion:

How did water interact with each of the different substances?

What result most surprised your group?

Explaining the Phenomenon

Water drops interact with each other and other substances as follows:

Construction paper: When a drop of water is placed on construction paper, it forms a shallow dome that flattens out very slowly as the water is absorbed by the paper. Construction paper has been coated with a substance called *sizing* that makes it less absorbent.

Newspaper: When a drop of water is placed on newspaper, it quickly flattens out as the water is absorbed by the paper. Under magnification, newspaper looks like a mass of fibers. The water molecules are attracted to the surface of these fibers and move along them.

Aluminum foil: When a drop of water is placed on aluminum, it forms a medium-sized dome. Water molecules *adhere,* or stick to, the atoms of aluminum. Because aluminum does not absorb water, the dome does not flatten out.

Wax paper: When a drop of water is placed on wax paper, it forms a high dome. Water molecules are repelled by wax molecules, but they *cohere* to each other. As they are pushed away by the wax molecules, the water molecules bunch up together in a pile.

Creating

1. Tell students that artists can use the interaction of water and wax in a painting process called *crayon-resist.* Crayon-resist is an art technique in which crayon is applied to paper and then covered with paint. Because wax repels water, the paint will not cover the crayoned part.

2. Tell students that they will be painting a picture that has water as its theme. Help students brainstorm picture ideas. Ask, "When you think of water, what pictures, or images, come to mind?" *(Umbrellas in the rain, river rapids, playing at the ocean, taking a bath, building a snowman, etc.)*

3. Demonstrate the procedure:

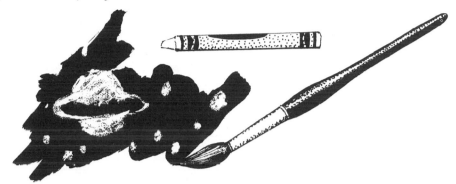

Use a pencil to sketch a picture on a sheet of white construction paper.

Use light-colored crayons to go over the pencil lines. Press hard with the crayons.

Paint over the crayoned areas with watercolor. Use broad, horizontal strokes as you paint.

As you work, repeatedly dip your brush into the watercolor pans to load it with color. Point out that adding more color to the paint on the paper will make the colors in the painting brighter, or more *intense.*

note
Show students how to rinse the brush with water before dipping it into a new color.

4. When students understand the procedure, distribute materials and have them begin. Circulate, and offer assistance as needed.

Evaluating

Display the dried paintings for everyone to see. Have students notice and compare the different ways their classmates used the technique of crayon-resist to depict the theme of water. Have them find examples of intense colors in their own and in their classmates' paintings.

Going Further

Have students generate a list of questions for further investigation. Examples of such questions are:

- *Why does oil float on water?* Have students use a balance scale to compare the weights of equal volumes of oil and water. They will notice that the oil weighs less. Students can weigh and compare equal volumes of such other liquids as alcohol or molasses. Have them record their observations in a journal or logbook.

■ *How can artists use oil and water?* Students can create a liquid sculpture that looks like an ocean in a bottle. Have them fill a bottle with a tight-fitting lid (such as an empty 1-liter soda bottle) half full of water. Have them add a few drops of food color and then pour on a layer of oil. Caution them to put the cap on tightly. They can then tip the bottle to put this sculpture in motion.

Additional Resources

Allison, Linda, and David Katz. "The Unmixables," *Gee, Wiz!* Boston: Little, Brown, 1983.

Strongin, Herb. "Red Drop, Green Drop," in *Science on a Shoestring.* Menlo Park, Calif.: Addison-Wesley, 1991.

Crime-Solving Chemistry

Overview

Who stole the painting from the art museum? In this simulation, students compare the interaction of three mystery substances with water in order to solve a burglary. One substance (powdered sugar) dissolves, the second (white powdered tempera) forms a suspension, and the third (plaster of Paris) reacts chemically with water to form a solid. After solving the mystery, students use the tempera paint and art chalk to create a drawing of the suspect.

Student Objectives

- predict and compare the interaction of three mystery substances with water.

- use art chalk and liquid tempera paint to create positive and negative shapes in a drawing.

Materials

- containers, such as cut-off milk cartons or plastic cups, 4 per group of 4 students

- safety goggles, 1 per student and 1 for the teacher

- white powdered tempera paint

- powdered sugar

- plaster of Paris

- masking tape

- water

- newspapers to cover work areas

- plastic teaspoons

- paper towels

- Logsheet 12: Who Stole the Painting? (page 173)

- Logsheet 13: Mystery Powders (page 174)

- dark-colored construction paper, approximately 12" x 18"

- pencils

- rulers

- art chalk

- water containers, such as cut-off milk cartons and coffee cans

Getting Ready

1. Draw a map of the crime scene on the chalkboard, as shown.

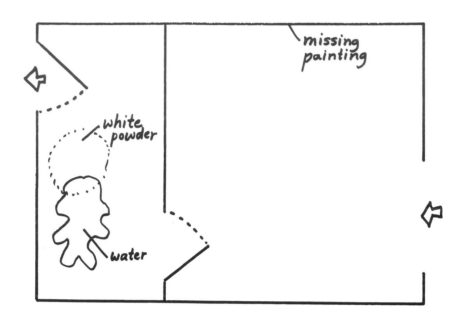

2. Prepare three containers for each group of four students. Place 2 level teaspoons of powdered white tempera in the first container. Place a piece of masking tape on this container, and label it "A." Place 2 level teaspoons of powdered sugar in the second container, and label it "B." Place 2 level teaspoons of plaster of Paris in the third container, and label it "C."

3. Fill one container with 1/2 cup of water for each group of four students.

4. Organize containers, teaspoons, paper towels, logsheets, art chalk, pencils, rulers, and colored construction paper for easy distribution during the lesson.

5. Cover work areas with newspaper.

note

Students should be organized into groups of four.

note

After students add water to the three mystery powders, they must wait at least 45 minutes before examining the three substances again. Teachers may want to divide the lesson into two sessions or may plan an alternate activity for students during the 45-minute waiting period.

Observing, Comparing, and Describing

1. Begin by having students share their knowledge of the steps involved in crime detection. The following questions are useful in guiding discussion:

What skills must a good detective possess? *(Keen observation, deduction, and communication skills)*

What does a detective look for at the scene of a crime? *(Clues)*

2. Tell students that they will be working in groups of four to solve a mystery. Distribute copies of the Logsheet 12: Who Stole the Painting? Read the scenario aloud with the class.

3. Distribute the containers of mystery powders to each group of four students. Tell students that substance A was found on the clothing of Prunella Bland. Substance B was found on the clothing of Emile Frost. Substance C was found on the clothing of Mrs. DeWitt. Record the information on the chalkboard as follows:

Substance A—Prunella Bland

Substance B—Emile Frost

Substance C—Mrs. DeWitt

4. Demonstrate the procedure:

Put on safety goggles. Carefully examine the three powders. Write a description of each in the first column on Logsheet 13: Mystery Powders.

Add 2 level teaspoons of water to each substance and stir vigorously for several minutes. Wipe the teaspoon clean with a paper towel after stirring.

Examine the three mixtures and write a description of each in the second column on the logsheet. Then, set your containers aside for a period of 45 minutes.

After 45 minutes, examine and compare the three mystery substances. Record your observations in the third column of the logsheet. Determine which of the three suspects is the criminal, and record your conclusion on the logsheet.

5. When students understand the procedure, distribute the logsheets and materials, and have them begin. Circulate, and offer assistance as needed.

Drawing Conclusions

Have students share their observations and conclusions. The following questions are useful in guiding discussion:

How did each of the three mystery powders react with water? *(Substance A formed a creamy white suspension; substance B dissolved into a translucent liquid; substance C formed a hard white solid.)*

What clues enabled you to identify the criminal?*(The thief exited through the supply room, knocking over two containers. One container held water, and the other held a mysterious white powder. When the water and the white powder mixed, they formed a hard white solid. Substance C is the only mystery powder to form a hard white solid. Since some of substance C was found on the clothing of Mrs. DeWitt, Mrs. DeWitt is the criminal.)*

SAFETY TIP

In accordance with your school safety policy, make safety goggles available for your students and direct students to wear it when using chemicals. Caution students against tasting any of the substances. Although these substances are nontoxic, students should never place an unknown substance in their mouths. Have students follow safety procedures and wash their hands thoroughly after completing the activity.

note

Students should be organized into pairs.

Explaining the Phenomenon

An *interaction* occurs when two or more things affect or change each other in some way. Each of the three powders interacted with water in a different way.

When water was added to the powdered tempera (substance A), a thick liquid was formed, called a *suspension*. A suspension occurs when solid particles seem to dissolve in a liquid, but they cannot pass through a fine membrane.

When water was added to the powdered sugar (substance B), most of the sugar dissolved. A liquid containing another substance dissolved in it is called a *solution*. A solution is a clear liquid mixture of two or more substances. The dissolved particles in solutions are able to pass through a very thin type of skin called a *membrane*.

When water was added to the plaster of Paris (substance C), a chemical reaction occurred. A *chemical reaction* occurs when atoms of one substance combine with atoms of another substance to form molecules.

Note

For further information about the chemical reaction of plaster of Paris and water, see "Chemical Reactions: Background Information" on page 71.

Creating

1. Tell students that they will next use two of the mystery substances, plaster of Paris and tempera paint, to create a drawing of the suspect. Show students the art chalk, and explain that it is composed of plaster of Paris (gypsum) and other substances.

2. Tell students that they will use the chalk and tempera paint to draw a picture of Mrs. DeWitt behind bars. Help students speculate about her physical appearance—height, coloring, shape, clothing, expression, and so on.

3. Demonstrate the procedure:

First, on dark-colored construction paper, draw a pencil sketch of Mrs. DeWitt standing in her jail cell. Then, use a ruler to draw vertical jail bars in front of her.

Use the art chalk to color Mrs. DeWitt and her surroundings, but leave the bars blank. Explain that the colored forms of Mrs. DeWitt and her surroundings form a *positive shape,* while the uncolored bars form a *negative shape.* Both positive and negative shapes interact to form a unified design.

To color, dip the art chalk into water before drawing on the dark construction paper. This will reduce the amount of chalk dust produced when drawing. To create a painterly effect, repeatedly dip the chalk into white tempera paint while drawing.

4. When students understand the procedure, distribute materials and have them begin. Circulate, and offer assistance as needed.

Evaluating

Display the finished chalk drawings for everyone to see. Have students notice the interaction between the positive and negative shapes in the drawings. Ask volunteers to discuss one thing they like about their drawing, and one thing they might do differently if they were to create a second drawing.

Going Further

Have students generate a list of questions for further investigation. Examples of such questions are:

Substances	Observations
salt	
talcum powder	
soil	
cane sugar	

- *What other kinds of substances dissolve in water?* Have students compare the solubility of the following substances: sodium chloride, or table salt (NaCl); talcum powder; garden soil; and sucrose, or cane sugar $(C_{12}H_{22}O_{11})$. Fill test tubes or other glass containers with 6 teaspoons of warm water. Add 1/2 teaspoon of each substance to a container of warm water, and stir. Have students complete a data sheet similar to the one shown.

  Line a funnel with filter paper. One by one, filter the mixtures by pouring them through the funnel into new containers. Be sure to use a fresh piece of filter paper each time. Have students record the results on the data sheet. Students will notice that salt and sugar pass easily through the filter paper, leaving no residue in the funnel. However, the talcum and garden soil both leave residues and are not true solutions.

- *What other substances react chemically with water?* Students can experiment by adding equal parts of water to equal amounts of such substances as flour and plaster of Paris. They will notice that the plaster of Paris reacts chemically with water and hardens but that the flour shows no reaction.

Additional Resources

Alexander, Kay. "Paper Cutouts," in *Learning to Look and Create: The Spectra Program, Grade Four*. Palo Alto, Calif.: Dale Seymour, 1988.

Mullin, Virginia L. *Chemistry Experiments for Children*. New York: Dover, 1968.

• •

Chemical Reactions: Background Information

Chemical reactions involve the formation or breaking of bonds between atoms or molecules. As atoms of different elements approach each other, their outermost electrons can interact, and a chemical reaction may occur.

When water freezes, it is still water. When it evaporates and forms vapor, it is still composed of the same atoms of hydrogen and oxygen. When salt dissolves in water, it is still salt. As soon as the water evaporates, the salt will form into white crystals again. Changes like these, which affect only the physical state of a substance without altering the structure of its molecules, are called *physical changes*.

When a wax candle burns, it is no longer wax. It would be impossible to "unburn" the candle and retrieve the original wax. When a piece of iron rusts, new molecules are formed from atoms of iron and atoms of oxygen. Changes like these, which alter the composition of compounds by adding, removing, or rearranging atoms, are called *chemical changes*.

Before we can understand how chemicals can react with each other, we must understand how atoms form ions. Certain atoms may tend to lose one or more of their outermost electrons. Other atoms have a tendency to gain electrons in addition to those they already possess. An atom that has lost or gained electrons is no longer a normal, neutral atom. An atom that has more than its normal share of negative electrons is negatively charged, and is called a *negative ion*. An atom that has less than its normal share of negative electrons is positively charged and is called a *positive ion*.

When an electron-losing atom, such as sodium, and an electron-gaining atom, such as chlorine come together, a *chemical reaction* can occur. An electron will leave the sodium atom and go over to the chlorine atom. The sodium atom, Na, becomes a sodium ion, Na+. The chlorine atom, Cl, becomes a chlorine ion, Cl–. Because these ions have opposite electrical charges, they attract each other and tend to cling together, forming molecules in a solid crystal of sodium chlorine, or table salt, NaCl.

Chemists use *formulas* to record reactions like the one discussed above. Na is the chemical symbol for sodium. Cl is the chemical symbol for chlorine. The following equation represents the chemical reaction of sodium and chlorine to form sodium chloride, or table salt:

$$Na + Cl \longrightarrow NaCl$$

No atom is ever lost in a chemical reaction. Atoms may be rearranged in various ways, but they are never destroyed and never created in ordinary chemical processes. This is the *law of conservation of matter*.

Capillary Action

Overview

How can water defy gravity? In this activity, students investigate the capillary action of water as they dip tissue paper into diluted food colors and observe the colored water flow upward. By folding the paper in different ways, students experiment to create a variety of colorful designs.

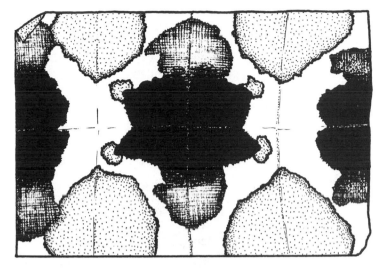

Student Objectives

- experiment to discover which of four kinds of paper is most porous.

- observe that water moves upward through tissue paper because its adhesive force is stronger than its cohesive force.

- use dyeing techniques with tissue paper and food colors to create symmetrical and repetitive designs.

Materials

- cotton ball
- large bottles of red, yellow, and blue food colors
- tablespoon
- measuring cup
- quart or liter container
- small containers to hold colored water, such as cut-off milk cartons or plastic cups
- papers such as construction paper, tissue paper, facial tissue, and newspaper
- hand lenses
- metric rulers
- Logsheet 14: Capillary Action (page 175)
- white or light-colored tissue paper
- newspapers to cover work areas

Getting Ready

1. Fill a quart or liter container with water. Add 1 tablespoon of blue food color. Pour 1/4 cup of blue-colored water into such small containers as clear plastic cups or cut-off milk cartons. Prepare one such container for every group of four students.

2. Gently pull a cotton ball until it stretches to a length of

approximately 4 inches. Place the cotton and a container of blue-colored water in a demonstration area at the front of the class.

3. Cut construction paper, newspaper, tissue paper, and facial tissue into strips approximately 1" x 4". For every group of students, prepare four strips of each kind. Organize the strips, containers of blue water, hand lenses, metric rulers, and logsheets for easy distribution during the "Observing, Comparing, and Describing" portion of the lesson.

4. For each group of four students, prepare three containers of colored water—red, yellow, and blue. Mix 1 tablespoon of a different food color with 2 tablespoons of water in each container.

5. Cut white or light colored tissue paper into rectangles approximately 9" x 12". Organize the tissue paper and containers of colored water for easy distribution during the "Creating" portion of the lesson.

6. Cover work areas with newspaper.

7. Select an area of the classroom where dyed papers can be set aside to dry.

note
Students should be organized into groups of four.

Observing, Comparing, and Describing

1. Begin by having students share their knowledge of gravity. The following questions are useful in guiding discussion:

When you hold a basketball and then let go, what happens to the ball? *(It falls down.)*

Why do things fall down rather than up? *(Gravity)*

What are examples of things that resist, or defy, gravity? *(Birds in flight, aircraft, etc.)*

Can water ever defy gravity and flow upward? *(By suction, as in a straw; by capillary action; by adhesion to another material, etc.)*

2. Show students the length of cotton. Ask them to predict what will happen to the blue-colored water when you dip one end of the cotton into it. *(The water will rise, or climb, upward.)*

3. Dip one end of the cotton into the water. Help students speculate about why the water climbed upward. The following questions are useful in guiding discussion:

Does water climb up such other materials as pencils, lengths of metal, or glass? *(Yes, but only to a small extent)*

On what kinds of materials does water climb? *(Porous materials)*

4. Tell students that they will be working in groups of four to compare four different kinds of paper: construction paper, newspaper, tissue paper, and facial tissue. They will dip each paper into water and observe how high the water climbs each one.

note
Inform students that the food coloring will stain hands and clothing. Remind them to work carefully to avoid spillage.

5. Distribute copies of Logsheet 14: Capillary Action. Tell students that as they complete the logsheet, each person should share ideas and observations with others in the group.

6. Demonstrate the procedure:

Use a hand lens to closely examine each paper. Notice its color, thickness, and texture. Write a description of each paper on the logsheet.

Dip one end of each paper strip in water for 60 seconds. Remove the strip, and measure the height of the water in millimeters. Record the height on the logsheet graph.

Write a paragraph on the back of the logsheet to summarize and explain your results.

7. When students understand the procedure, distribute the materials, and have them begin. Circulate, and offer assistance.

Drawing Conclusions

Have students share their results. The following questions are useful in guiding discussion:

What happened? *(Water climbed highest in facial tissue and least high in construction paper.)*

How did the structure of each paper affect how high the water traveled? *(The more porous the paper, the more small vertical spaces it had, the more easily and quickly the water climbed upward.)*

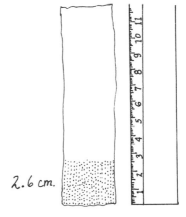

2.6 cm.

On what other sorts of materials might water climb easily? *(Cotton and other porous fabrics, loose soils, etc.)*

Explaining the Phenomenon

1. Explain that water rises through porous materials because its *adhesive force* (its tendency to stick to other things) is stronger than its *cohesive force* (its tendency to stick to itself).

2. Such porous materials as cotton or tissue paper contain many small vertical spaces into which water can rise. In small tubes, where there is a lot of surface area for water to adhere to, water can climb a great distance. This ability, called *capillary action,* or *capillarity,* helps water climb up tree trunks and plant stems.

note

For more information about capillary action, see "Capillary Action: Background Information" on page 77.

Creating

1. Tell students that artists use the adhesive properties of water to create designs by dyeing fabrics or papers.

2. Demonstrate the procedure:

Fold a rectangle of tissue paper in half, and then fold it in half again. Grasp the folded paper by one corner with thumb and forefinger.

Dip one corner of the paper into a container of colored water until the color rises approximately 1" into the paper. Remove the paper from the colored water.

Turn the folded paper, and dip another corner into a container of a second color. Allow the color to rise approximately 1" into the paper, and then remove the paper.

Fold the paper in half yet again, and dip another corner into a container of the third color. Remove the paper, and carefully open the folds to expose the entire sheet.

3. Have students notice the resulting design. Explain that *repetition* is an element of design in which an artist uses repeating colors, lines, shapes, or designs. Ask students to find examples of repetition in the design.

4. Explain that *symmetry* is an element of design in which an artist achieves a sense of balance by creating identical or similar colors, lines, or shapes on either side of the center. Have students find examples of symmetry in the design.

5. Tell students that different kinds of folds will yield different kinds of designs and that they should experiment with a variety of folds to create different effects.

6. When students understand the procedure, distribute the containers of colored water and tissue paper. As they dye their papers, circulate, and offer assistance as needed.

Evaluating

After the finished designs have dried, display them in the classroom. Ask students to look for examples of repetition and symmetry in the designs. Have students compare the different kinds of designs achieved by various methods of folding the papers.

Going Further

Have students generate a list of questions for further investigation. Examples of such questions are:

■ *What kinds of fabrics are most suitable for dyeing?* Have students bring in scraps of such fabrics as cotton, denim, polyester, rayon, and velvet. Cut the fabric scraps into narrow strips, and have students dip the ends of the strips into colored water. Have students record the results in a journal or logbook.

■ *How does water climb plant stems?* Obtain celery stalks with leaves turning yellow. Place them in food color solution. Leave the stalks in bright light for a few hours, and then have students observe how the colored water has risen to the leaves. Have students observe cross slices of celery to discover that the celery "strings" are really pipes, or conducting tissue.

■ *How does water climb in soils?* Have students compare the capillarity of soils. Students may prepare three funnels with gauze taped or tied to the bottom of the mouth. Pack one with sand, another with clay, and the third with soil rich in humus. Fill three jars with water, and place each funnel on top of a jar so that the stem of the funnel reaches the water level. Have students watch the rate of water absorption in each funnel. Through which kind of soil does water rise readily by capillarity? Students may record their observations in a journal or logbook.

Additional Resources

Lowery, Lawrence F. "Inorganic Matter," in *The Everyday Science Sourcebook.* Palo Alto, Calif.: Dale Seymour, 1985.

Pratt VanCleave, Janice. *Biology for Every Kid.* New York: Wiley & Sons, 1990.

● ●

Capillary Action: Background Information

In a teacup, tea climbs up the string of the tea bag and over the edge, defying the force of gravity. Dip the corner of a paper towel into a puddle of water on the table, and watch the water climb. Look at a glass of water, and you will see that the water lifts itself up a bit all around the edge. The forces that make this happen are the forces between the molecules of water.

Molecules of all kinds attract each other. The molecules within a liquid attract each other, and if the liquid comes in contact with a solid, the molecules of the liquid and the molecules of the solid attract each other as well. The attraction between molecules of the same kind is called *cohesion.* The attraction between molecules of a different kind is called *adhesion.*

Such porous materials as cotton or tissue paper contain many small, vertical spaces into which water can rise. In small tubes, where there is a lot of surface area for water to adhere to, water can climb a great distance. This ability, called *capillary action,* or *capillarity,* helps water climb up tree trunks and plant stems. When you light a candle, the heat of the candle's flame melts the wax at the top. Then capillary action pulls the melted wax up through the wick, where it burns in the flame. Capillary action also holds water in the topmost layers of soil. When a farmer plows a field, it is not just to control weeds, but to conserve water as well. Cultivation loosens the settled soil, adding large air spaces. These spaces interfere with the capillary action that causes water to rise to the surface and evaporate.

Paper Chromatography

Overview

How does water interact with various inks? This activity begins with a simulation in which students use the technique of paper chromatography to determine which black pen was used to create an art forgery. During their investigations, students observe that some inks are soluble in water but that others are not. After solving the mystery, students use marking pens and water to create drawings with contrasting sharp and fuzzy lines.

Student Objectives

- use the technique of paper chromatography to separate and compare the pigments that are mixed to make black inks.

- use water-soluble markers, water, and brushes to create drawings that show a contrast between sharp and fuzzy lines.

Materials

- white paper towels, round coffee filters, or other absorbent paper, approximately 100

- scissors, 1 pair

- water

- small containers to hold water, such as cut-off milk cartons, plastic cups, etc.

- masking tape

- black felt-tip pens, 9 or more, of varied brands

- rulers, 1 per group of 4 students and 3 per investigation area

- half-gallon milk cartons cut lengthwise to serve as water troughs, 2 per investigation area

- water-soluble markers, black or colored, 1 or more per student

- construction paper, white, approximately 9" x 12"

- brushes, small

- newspapers to cover work areas

- Logsheet 15: Paper Chromatography (page 176), 1 per group of 4 students

Getting Ready

1. Cut paper towels into strips approximately 1" x 4". You will need seven strips per group of four students.

2. For each group of four students, pour 1/2 inch of water into the bottom of a cut-off milk carton.

3. Tape numbers on the black felt-tip pens so that the pens can be easily identified.

4. With each pen, conduct a chromatography test. Use the following procedure:

Draw a horizontal line across a paper strip about 1 1/2 inches from the bottom.

Tape the top of the strip to a ruler with masking tape.

Set the ruler across the top of the milk carton so that the paper strip hangs down and just touches the water. The ink line should be at least 1/2 inch above the water.

Remove the paper strip when the water has risen about three-quarters of the length of the paper.

5. Compare the test strips. Nine pens usually yield four or more patterns. Some pens will not create a pattern at all (but include these in the collection anyway). Select one pen with a unique color pattern to be the Mystery Marker. Select an additional five pens to use in the lesson so that you have six pens in all.

6. With the Mystery Marker, draw a line 1 1/2 inches above the bottom of several test strips—one for each group of four students. These test strips will serve as pieces of the art forgery. Organize the test strips, logsheets, and water containers for easy distribution to student groups during the "Observing, Comparing, and Describing" portion of the lesson.

7. Prepare one table or investigation area for each pen. At each area, place several lengths of masking tape, a pen, and paper strips. Tape two or three rulers lengthwise across a water trough so that student pairs can tape their strips to hang from the rulers into the water.

8. Organize water-soluble markers, construction paper, brushes, and newspapers for easy distribution during the "Creating" portion of the lesson.

Observing, Comparing, and Describing

1. Begin by having students share their knowledge of the steps involved in crime detection. The following questions are useful in guiding discussion:

What skills must a good detective possess? *(Keen observation, deduction, and communication skills)*

What does a detective look for at the scene of a crime? *(Clues)*

What professionals might a detective consult during the course of an investigation? *(Doctors, forensic chemists, etc.)*

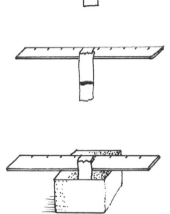

note
Students should be organized into groups of four.

2. Tell students that police detectives often work closely with forensic chemists. A *forensic chemist* is a scientist who uses chemistry to solve legal problems.

3. Explain that the police need help in determining who might have forged a famous drawing. The drawing was created with a black felt-tip pen on white paper. Several suspects have been identified, and their pens have been confiscated. (Show students the pens.) Tell students their job is to discover which of the confiscated pens was used to create the forgery.

4. Tell students that they will be using *chromatography,* a technique used for separating substances from a mixture, to identify the criminal's pen.

5. Distribute one test strip to each group of four students, and explain that the strip is a piece of the forged drawing.

6. Distribute one cut-off milk carton filled with 1/2 inch of water, one ruler, a copy of Logsheet 15: Paper Chromatography, and a length of masking tape to each group of students. Have each group select one member to tape test strips on the logsheet and record the group's conclusions.

7. Demonstrate the procedure:

Attach the top of the paper test strip to a ruler with masking tape.

Set the ruler across the top of the milk carton so that the paper strip hangs down and just touches the water. The ink line should be at least 1/2 inch above the water.

Remove the paper strip when the water has traveled about three-quarters of the way up. Tape the test strip to the "Forgery Sample" area of the logsheet.

8. When students understand the procedure, have them prepare the test sample.

9. Tell students that they next will use chromatography to discover which pen was used to create the forgery. Explain that they will test a different pen at each station, or investigation area, in the room.

10. Demonstrate the procedure:

Go to one of the investigation areas. Use the pen to draw a horizontal line across a paper strip about 1 1/2 inches from the bottom.

Write your names at the top of the strip, along with the number of the pen being tested.

Tape the strip to a ruler and suspend it in water as before.

Select another investigation area and repeat the procedure there with a different pen. Circulate to each area until you have tested each pen.

11. When students understand the procedure, have them begin. Circulate, and offer assistance as needed.

note

Students may need to fold over one end of the test strip to fit it on the logsheet.

note

Remind students to write their names and the number of each pen on the test strip.

12. After students have completed their tests, have them collect
their chromatograms from each investigation area and tape
them to their logsheets.

Drawing Conclusions

1. Ask students to carefully examine and compare their
chromatograms to determine which pen they think was used to
create the forgery. Have students record their conclusions on
the logsheets.

2. Have students share their results. The following questions are
useful in guiding discussion:

Did different groups have different results? What could cause
this? *(Variation in the amount of ink applied to the paper,
the amount of time the paper was left in water, etc.)*

Which ink contained the greatest number of pigments?
(Answers will vary.)

How many different patterns were produced? *(Answers will
vary.)*

Which ink traveled the farthest? *(The ink containing the
lightest pigment particles)*

Explaining the Phenomenon

The technique of chromatography separates substances from a
mixture, such as marking pen ink. Each mixture produces its own
color pattern, called a *chromatogram*. The colors that students
observed are the pigments that were mixed together to make black
ink.

When we write with a pen or marker, the liquid part evaporates and
leaves just the color behind on the paper. Some inks are a
combination of two or more coloring substances. These colors can
be separated by adding a solvent such as water. A *solvent* is a
liquid capable of dissolving other substances.

When the water travels up the test strip, it comes into contact with
the dried color. It loosens or dissolves the coloring molecules in
the ink and carries them up the strip. Different colors are carried
faster and farther than others, for a number of reasons, including
the type of solvent used and the weight and size of the pigment
particles.

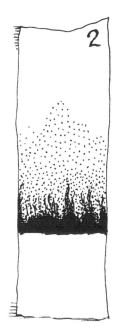

Creating

1. Tell students that artists use solvents such as water to create
interesting effects when drawing with colored markers. Explain
that they will be using water and markers to create drawings
that show a contrast between sharp and fuzzy lines.

2. Define *contrast* as "the use of differences in artwork." Examples include light against dark, bright against dull, large against small, and sharp against fuzzy.

3. Demonstrate the procedure:

Cover the work area with a sheet of newspaper.

Use one or more markers to draw a picture on white construction paper. Possible subjects include fantasy animals, monsters, and a rainy day.

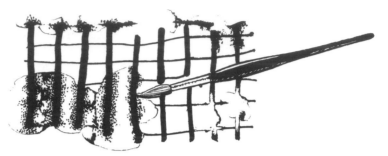

Dip a brush into water and lightly touch the brush to some of the lines in the drawing. Because the markers are water soluble, the color will spread, and the lines will become soft and fuzzy.

Remind students to leave other lines dry so that the finished drawing will show a contrast between sharp and fuzzy lines.

4. When students understand the procedure, distribute newspapers, construction paper, markers, brushes, and have them begin. (They can use the water containers that were distributed earlier in the lesson.) Circulate, and offer assistance as needed. Encourage students to experiment by adding color to the wet areas on the paper.

note
Students should be organized into pairs or small groups.

Evaluating

Display the dried drawings for the class to see. Ask students to discuss the contrast between the lines that were wet with water and those that were not.

Going Further

Have students generate a list of questions for further investigation. Examples of such questions are:

SAFETY TIP

In accordance with your school safety policy, make safety goggles available for students and direct students to wear them when using chemicals. Remind students not to taste chemicals or bring them into contact with their eyes or skin and to wash their hands thoroughly after completing the activity.

- *Why did some of the pens fail to create patterns?* The inks in some markers will not dissolve in water. Have students experiment with such other solvents as rubbing alcohol, vinegar, and ditto fluid (denatured alcohol) in a well-ventilated area to discover which solvent will cause pigments in the ink to travel.

- *What other kinds of pigments or coloring can be separated by using the technique of paper chromatography?* Students can use chromatography to test plant pigments. Apply plant pigment to a paper strip by placing the plant sample on the strip and crushing the sample firmly with the edge of a scissor or butter knife. Repeat this several times to apply as much pigment as possible. Experiment with flower petals, purple cabbage, spinach, and other plants. Have students use a variety of solvents to discover which cause plant pigments to travel (vinegar, rubbing alcohol, and ditto fluid).

Students can discover the solvent required and the number of pigments that can be separated from each plant. Have students record their findings in a journal or logbook.

Additional Resources

Allison, Linda, and David Katz. "Exploding Colors: The Science of Chromatography," in *Gee, Wiz!* Boston: Little, Brown, 1983.

Barber, Jacqueline. *Crime Lab Chemistry,* in the *Great Explorations in Math and Science* (GEMS) series. Berkeley, Calif.: Lawrence Hall of Science, University of California, 1985.

Crystals

Overview

How does water affect the appearance of some crystals? Water molecules, when included in crystals, make up *water of crystallization,* also called *water of hydration.* In this activity, students compare Epsom salt crystals (magnesium sulfate) before and after adding water. Using watercolors and epsom salt solution, they create paintings that reveal beautiful patterns of colored, needlelike crystals.

Student Objectives

- observe that water molecules interact with the molecules of magnesium sulfate to make up *water of crystallization,* also called *water of hydration.*

- use watercolor techniques to create a painting.

Materials

- safety goggles, 1 per student and 1 for the teacher
- 1 lb Epsom salts (magnesium sulfate)
- small shallow containers or trays, such as plastic foam trays, coffee can lids, or aluminum pie pans, 1 per student pair
- 1/4 teaspoon measure
- 1/2-gal water container
- watercolor sets with brushes
- white construction paper
- water containers, such as cut-off milk cartons, plastic cups
- wax crayons
- paper towels
- hand lenses
- Logsheet 16: Crystals (page 177)
- newspapers to cover work areas
- (optional) Logsheet 17: Constructing Crystalline Shapes (page 178)
- (optional) Logsheet 18: Constructing More Crystalline Shapes (page 179)
- (optional) scissors, 1 per student
- (optional) glue

SAFETY TIP

Instruct students to wear safety goggles when handling chemicals in accordance with your school's policy. Remind students never to taste chemicals during a science investigation, and to wash their hands thoroughly before leaving class. In this case, Epsom salts are nontoxic unless they are ingested in doses exceeding 4 level tsp.

Getting Ready

1. Obtain Epsom salts from a drugstore.

2. Prepare one shallow container for every two students. Use such containers as plastic foam trays, coffee can lids, or aluminum pie pans. Place 1/4 teaspoon of Epsom salts in each container.

3. Prepare a 1/2- gallon solution of Epsom salts and water in a large container. Mix 1 part Epsom salts with 3 parts water, and stir until the salt is dissolved. Pour the solution into water containers—one per student pair.

4. Arrange watercolors and brushes, paper, containers, crayons, paper towels, hand lenses, and logsheets for easy distribution during the lesson.

5. Set aside classroom space for the watercolors to dry undisturbed.

6. Cover work areas with newspapers.

note

Students should be organized into groups of four.

note

You might want to divide this lesson into two sessions or plan an alternative activity while students are waiting for the watercolors to dry (about one hour). For example, in the first session, students may investigate the dry Epsom salts and create watercolor paintings. In the second session, students may investigate the crystals in the finished paintings and draw conclusions.

Observing, Comparing, and Describing

1. Begin by having students share their knowledge of crystals. The following questions are useful in guiding discussion:

What are crystals? *(Solid pieces of matter composed of many atoms arranged in patterns)*

What do crystals look like? *(Each crystalline substance has its own geometric shape.)*

Where are crystals found? *(In rocks, minerals, and ice)*

2. Explain that a *crystal* is a solid piece of matter composed of many atoms arranged in patterns. A substance that is composed of crystals is called *crystalline*. Each crystalline substance has its own geometric shape and pattern. For instance, snowflakes, which are melting ice crystals, have a 6-sided, or hexagonal, pattern. Table salt crystals look like little cubes.

3. Tell students that they will be working in groups of four to investigate a crystalline substance called Epsom salts.

4. Distribute copies of Logsheet 16: Crystals. Tell students that as they complete the top portion of the logsheet, each person should share observations with others in the group.

5. Explain the procedure: First, examine the substance with the hand lens and describe the shape, color, and size of its crystals on the logsheet. Next, draw a quick sketch of the crystals.

6. When students understand the procedure, distribute the samples of Epsom salts and the hand

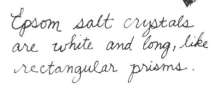

Epsom salt crystals are white and long, like rectangular prisms.

lenses. Circulate, and offer assistance as students investigate.

7. Tell students that the next step is to see what happens when watercolor is added to the Epsom salts and then allowed to evaporate. This step will involve painting with watercolors and an Epsom salts solution.

Creating

1. Tell students that they will make watercolor paintings using an Epsom salt solution instead of water. Show students the solution, and explain that it was made by mixing 1 part of Epsom salts with 3 parts of water.

2. Tell students that after the water has evaporated from the paintings, they will examine them to see whether any residue has been left and whether any crystals have formed.

3. Demonstrate how to use a wax crayon to divide the white construction paper into separate areas for painting. This can be done by drawing a grid or by drawing curving, crisscrossing lines. Explain that the purpose of the wax lines is to separate different colors of paint.

4. Dip the brush into the Epsom salts solution, mix it with one color, and paint an area on the paper. Paint only the area *inside* the crayon lines. Use a generous amount of solution so that the painted area is quite wet, like a puddle.

5. Next, show students how to rinse the brush in water and dry it with a paper towel. Then, dip it in solution again and paint another area with a different color.

6. Distribute materials so that students can begin to work. Circulate, and offer assistance when necessary.

7. Have students carefully carry finished paintings to a place in the room where they can dry undisturbed.

Observing, Comparing, and Describing

When the watercolors have dried, ask students to examine them carefully with the hand lenses. Have them write a description and draw a quick sketch of the crystals on the bottom portion of the logsheet.

Drawing Conclusions

Have students share their observations. The following questions are useful in guiding observation:

What do you notice about the dried watercolors? *(They are covered with a thin crust of crystals.)*

What do the crystals look like? *(Thin and needlelike)*

How are the crystals different from the dry Epsom salts crystals you observed earlier? *(Larger, more transparent)* How are they similar? *(The shape is the same.)*

How long is the longest crystal you can find? How short is the shortest? *(Answers will vary.)*

Explaining the Phenomenon

Some crystals include molecules of water along with their atoms. The water molecules affect the appearance of the crystal. When water is added and then allowed to evaporate, the appearance of the crystals changes.

The chemical name for Epsom salts is magnesium sulfate. Its chemical formula is written as follows:

$$MgSO_4 \cdot 7H_2O$$

The number 7 in the formula indicates that when water is added to magnesium sulfate, 7 water molecules combine with each molecule of magnesium sulfate. The water molecules become part of the crystal structure in an interaction with the compound. This interaction is called *water of crystallization,* or *water of hydration.*

Crystals will grow larger in some paint colors than in others. This is because each paint color is made with a different pigment, or coloring substance. Some pigments are lighter than others, being composed of smaller particles. Crystals grow larger in solutions containing small, light particles.

Going Further

Have students generate a list of questions for further investigation. Examples of such questions are:

- *What are the different shapes of various crystals?* Students can use Logsheet 17: Constructing Crystalline Shapes and Logsheet 18: Constructing More Crystalline Shapes, to make a set of the basic crystalline shapes. Have students cut out the patterns and glue the tabs together. Students can then work in groups to sort the shapes by similarities and differences.

- *What kinds of rocks have crystals?* Have students compare several examples of granite, basalt, and obsidian rocks. By examining the rocks with hand lenses, students will observe differences in the crystalline structure.

Additional Resources

Lowery, Lawrence F. "Inorganic Matter," in *The Everyday Science Sourcebook.* Palo Alto, Calif.: Dale Seymour, 1985.

Mullin, Virginia L. *Chemistry Experiments for Children.* New York: Dover, 1961.

note

Teachers of younger students may wish to omit the chemical formula from this part of the lesson.

Inventing a Better Chalk

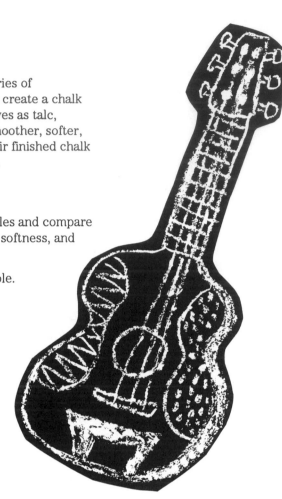

Overview

How can you invent a better kind of art chalk? In this series of
investigations, students begin by using plaster of Paris to create a chalk
control sample. Next, they experiment with such additives as talc,
cornstarch, and food color as they attempt to create a smoother, softer,
more brightly colored chalk. Students then field-test their finished chalk
pieces by drawing with them on dark construction paper.

Student Objectives

- evaluate the performance of experimental chalk samples and compare
  with a control sample, using such criteria as strength, softness, and
  intensity of color.

- keep organized records of recipes for each chalk sample.

- use chalk to create a line drawing on dark-colored
  construction paper.

Materials

- plaster of Paris, 4 lbs

- small disposable containers, such as cut-off milk
  cartons or paper cups, 2 per student

- plastic teaspoons

- modeling clay, 1 fist-sized lump per student pair

- large wax crayon segments

- pencils

- paper towels

- dark-colored construction paper, 18" x 24", several sheets per student

- Logsheet 19: Inventing a Better Chalk (page 180), 1 per student pair

- masking tape

- cornstarch, 1 lb

- talc, approximately 9 oz

- food coloring, 3 large bottles of red, yellow, and blue

- droppers, 3 per group of 4 students

- newspapers to cover work areas

- water

- (optional) gum tragacanth

Getting Ready

1. Obtain plaster of Paris from a local arts and crafts store or from a local building materials supply store. Obtain cornstarch, food coloring, and talc (baby talcum powder) from a local grocery store.

2. For each group of four students, provide a container with 1/2 cup of plaster of Paris and a second container with 1/2 cup of water.

3. Organize containers of water and plaster of Paris, teaspoons, empty disposable containers, modeling clay, large crayon pieces, pencils, logsheets, and paper towels for easy distribution during the initial investigation.

4. Cover work areas with newspaper.

5. Set aside an area of the classroom where chalk pieces can dry undisturbed.

6. For each subsequent investigation, prepare five containers for each group of four students. In the first container, place 1/4 cup of talc. In the second container, place 1/4 cup of cornstarch. Label the containers by writing the name of the substance on a strip of masking tape and attaching it to the appropriate container. In the remaining three containers, place 1 teaspoon each of red, yellow, and blue food coloring. Place one dropper in each container of food coloring.

note

Making the control sample of chalk in the first session will take 15–20 minutes. The chalk then must harden for 40 minutes and dry overnight. Each subsequent chalk sample will require a 15–25-minute session, followed by a period in which the chalk is allowed to harden and dry.

note

Students should be organized into pairs.

Observing, Comparing, and Describing

1. Begin by having students share their knowledge of chalk. Hold up a piece of chalkboard chalk for everyone to see. The following questions are useful in guiding discussion:

What is this used for? *(Writing on chalkboards, drawing pictures, marking on cloth, etc.)*

What is it made of? *(Antidust chalk is made of calcium carbonate, or limestone; regular chalk is made of gypsum or calcium sulfate.)*

How is it made? *(Chalk made of gypsum is made by combining gypsum and water.)*

What qualities must a good piece of chalk have? *(Strength, softness, brightness)*

What qualities would a poor piece of chalk have? *(Brittleness, hardness, dullness)*

2. Tell students that their task is to invent a good piece of chalk. Define a good piece of chalk as having the following qualities:

Strength—It does not splinter or shatter; it stays in one piece when you draw with it.

Softness—It is soft enough to deposit a good amount of color onto paper; it moves smoothly and easily over the paper's surface.

Intensity—Its colors are bright and easily seen.

3. Tell students that before they can begin experimenting, they must first make a piece of chalk to serve as a control sample. Later, students can compare their experimental chalk samples with the control sample to determine whether they are of better quality.

4. Tell students that they will be working in pairs to create the control sample. Demonstrate the procedure:

Shape a lump of modeling clay into an ovoid.

Place the clay ovoid on a table surface. Press a piece of thick wax crayon horizontally down into the clay ovoid. Press the crayon into the clay until the top side of the crayon is level with the clay surface.

Gently loosen the clay around the edges of the crayon. Remove the crayon. The clay should contain a long, deep, rectangular trough.

Use a plastic teaspoon to measure 4 level teaspoons of plaster of Paris into an empty disposable container. Use the side of a pencil to level off the plaster before adding it to the container.

Add 2 teaspoons of water, and stir until the mixture is smooth. Wipe the spoon clean with a paper towel.

Pour the mixture into the clay trough. Set the trough aside so that it can harden (in about 40 minutes).

5. When students understand the procedure, distribute the materials and have them begin. Circulate, and offer assistance as needed.

6. After students have set aside the control samples to harden, distribute copies of Logsheet 19: Inventing a Better Chalk. Have students write the recipe for the control sample in the appropriate space:

2 parts plaster of Paris

1 part water

7. Later, after at least 40 minutes or before going home for the day, have students gently pry the clay away from the hardened chalk sample, remove the damp chalk, and place it on a sheet of paper towel to dry. Have students write their names on the paper towel.

Drawing Conclusions

1. After the chalk samples have dried, distribute small squares of dark construction paper, and ask students to test their chalk by drawing several strokes on the paper. Remind students to evaluate the chalk by carefully observing the following qualities:

Strength—It does not splinter or shatter; it stays in one piece when you draw with it.

Softness—It is soft enough to deposit a good amount of color onto paper; it moves smoothly and easily over the paper's surface.

Intensity—Its colors are bright and easily seen.

2. Have students write their evaluations on the logsheets. They should also staple or tape their sample drawings to the logsheets.

3. Ask students to share their evaluations. (They probably will have noticed that the chalk has strength but not softness and that its intensity is moderate.)

4. Have students use pencil to write their initials on the control sample and set it aside for later use.

Explaining the Phenomenon

The hardening of the plaster of Paris is the result of a chemical reaction between the plaster of Paris and water. Plaster of Paris is made by roasting calcium sulfate (gypsum, $CaSO_4 \cdot 2H_2O$) at 212–374 degrees Fahrenheit. At that temperature, the calcium sulfate loses three-fourths of its water of crystallization and becomes $CaSO_4 \cdot 1/2\ H_2O$, the familiar plaster of Paris. When mixed with water, it takes up the one and a half parts of water again and, when dried, hardens to a solid mass. This mass will remain a solid and will no longer react with water.

Observing, Comparing, and Describing

1. Tell students that since the 18th century, those who make art chalk have often added other substances to plaster of Paris in order to increase its softness and color intensity.

2. Show students the talc, cornstarch, plaster of Paris, water, and food coloring. Challenge them to experiment with various combinations of these ingredients to discover a recipe for a better chalk—one with the most strength, softness, and color intensity.

3. Tell students that two pairs will work together as a group of four. Have them discuss ways in which the task could be divided up. (One pair might experiment with combinations of plaster of Paris and talc while the other pair experiments with combinations of plaster of Paris and cornstarch, and so on.)

4. Tell students that they must write the recipe for each new chalk on the logsheet.

5. When students understand the procedure, distribute materials and have them begin. Circulate, and offer assistance as needed. Encourage teams to try as many different combinations as they can.

6. After the experimental samples have hardened and dried, have groups create drawing samples and then compare and evaluate the results. Have them record their evaluations on the logsheets and attach a drawing sample of each chalk.

Our chalk is very strong and hard! It is not very intense, and it doesn't move well on the paper.

note

For more information about chemical reactions, see "Chemical Reactions: Background Information" on page 71.

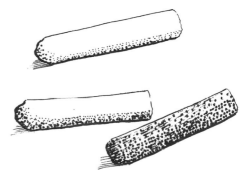

7. Once a group has selected the best recipe for a better chalk, have each group member use the recipe to make a piece. Each piece of chalk should be a different color.

Drawing Conclusions

Ask each group to share the results with the class. The following questions are useful in guiding discussion:

How did each group divide up the task? *(Answers will vary.)*

What combinations of substances did each group try first, second, third, and so on? *(Answers will vary.)*

What combinations were regarded as failures? *(Probably combinations containing plaster of Paris in quantities smaller than 50% of the dried material)*

What combination did each group find most successful? *(Probably combinations containing plaster of Paris in quantities greater than 50% of the dried material; combinations in which food coloring was used in place of water)*

Creating

1. Tell students to use their final pieces of chalk to draw a line drawing.

2. Demonstrate how to dip chalk in water to reduce the amount of chalk dust produced while drawing.

3. When students understand the procedure, distribute colored construction paper and water, and have them begin. Circulate, and offer assistance as needed.

Evaluating

Display the finished drawings for everyone to see. Have students compare the color intensity of the various drawings.

Going Further

Have students generate a list of questions for further investigation. Examples of such questions are:

- *What other kinds of liquids can be used in making chalk?* Eighteenth-century artists' guides are filled with recipes for chalks in which each pigment is mixed with a different binding material. Examples of binders included such homely materials as milk, stale beer, and oatmeal water. Students can experiment with such liquids as milk, honey, and egg whites. Have students compare and evaluate the results and record their findings in a journal or logbook.

- *How are pastels made?* Students can make art pastels by combining a pigment such as talc with a binding material. A commonly used binding medium is 48 oz water and 1 oz gum tragacanth (powdered). Gum tragacanth is available at most art supply stores. Have students mix the pigment with the binder until it is smooth and of the consistency of putty. They can then roll it into sticks with their hands on a layer of newspaper, holding their fingers parallel to the sticks, not at right angles to them. Set the sticks on a sheet of newspaper and allow them to dry at normal room temperature for two days.

Additional Resources

Alexander, Kay. "Rembrandt Van Rijn, Painter of Character," and "Marc Chagall's Fantastic Dreams," in *Learning to Look and Create: The Spectra Program, Grade Six.* Palo Alto, Calif.: Dale Seymour, 1988.

> **SAFETY TIP**
> Remind students not to taste the gum tragacanth and to wash their hands thoroughly after completing the activity.

Acids and Bases

Overview

How do acids and bases interact with each other? Students discover the answer to this question as they experiment by applying wet soap (a base) and lemon juice (an acid) to goldenrod paper. They observe that the paper turns bright red-orange where it is touched by the soap. When students apply lemon juice to the red-orange lines, the lines slowly disappear. After a discussion of their observations and an explanation of the phenomenon, students use soap and lemon juice to create designs having both positive and negative shapes.

Student Objectives

- observe that goldenrod xerographic paper is an indicator.

- observe than an acid can neutralize a base.

- use soap and lemon juice on goldenrod paper to create a design having both positive and negative shapes.

Materials

- safety goggles

- goldenrod xerographic paper, 100 sheets

- small containers, such as plastic cups or cut-off milk cartons

- lemon juice or vinegar, 2 cups

- water

- small bars of soap

- cotton swabs

- Logsheet 20: Acids and Bases (page 181)

- small-bristle brushes

- crayons, several per student

- newspapers to cover work areas

Getting Ready

1. Most brands of goldenrod xerographic paper will turn a deep red-orange in the presence of such alkalis as soap or baking soda solution. Obtain 100 sheets of goldenrod xerographic paper from your school or local printing supply store. Goldenrod is a deep, yellow-orange color. To be sure the dye in the paper contains an indicator, test the paper using the following procedure:

   Moisten one end of a piece of bar soap with water, and use the soap to draw several lines across the paper.

   If the paper contains an indicator, the lines will rapidly turn a deep red-orange color.

If there was no change in color, this type of paper does not contain an indicator. Try a deeper shade of yellow-orange paper from the same manufacturer, or try to obtain some sheets of goldenrod paper from a different manufacturer.

2. Obtain enough bars of soap so that each student can have one. Students can bring soaps from home to use.

3. For each group of four students, pour 1/4 cup of lemon juice or vinegar into a small container. Fill another container with water.

4. Organize goldenrod paper, logsheets, containers of lemon juice and water, safety goggles, small bar soaps, cotton swabs, brushes, and crayons for easy distribution during the lesson.

5. Cover work areas with newspaper.

Observing, Comparing, and Describing

1. Begin by having students share their knowledge of acids and bases. The following questions are useful in guiding discussion:

What is an acid? *(A sour-tasting substance; a substance containing hydrogen ions.)*

Where might we find acids in nature? *(In some fruits, such as orange, lemon, and tomato, in some rain or ground water, in some soils, in the stomach, etc.)*

What is a base? *(The chemical opposite of an acid; a substance containing hydroxyl ions.)*

What kinds of substances are basic, or alkaline? *(Such substances as ammonia and baking soda)*

2. Show students a bar of soap, and identify it as a base. Show students the lemon juice or vinegar, and identify it as an acid.

3. Tell students that they will be working in groups of four to investigate the interaction of soap and vinegar with goldenrod paper.

4. Distribute copies of Logsheet 20: Acids and Bases. Tell students that as they each complete the logsheet, they should share ideas and observations with others in the group.

5. Explain the procedure:

Dip one end of a bar soap into water, and draw several lines on a sheet of goldenrod paper. Observe the goldenrod paper carefully. Write your observations on the logsheet.

Dip one end of a cotton swab into lemon juice or vinegar, and draw several lines on the goldenrod paper. Write your observations on the logsheet.

Experiment to discover what happens when lemon juice is applied over the soap lines on the paper, and vice versa. Write your observations on the logsheet.

note

Students should be organized into groups of four.

SAFETY TIP

In accordance with your school safety policy, make safety goggles available for your students and have students wear them when using acids. Remind students not to taste chemicals or bring them into contact with their eyes or skin and to wash their hands thoroughly after completing the activity. Lemon juice and vinegar are irritants to the eyes but are otherwise safe to use.

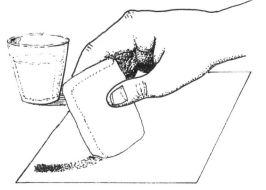

6. When students understand the procedure, distribute the materials, and have them begin. Circulate, and offer assistance as needed.

Drawing Conclusions

Have students share their observations. The following questions are useful in guiding discussion:

What happens when the acid is applied to the paper? *(Nothing)*

What happens when the base is applied to the paper? *(Deep red-orange lines appear.)*

What happens when the acid is applied to the paper and then covered with the base? *(As more and more soap is applied over the lemon juice or vinegar, red-orange lines slowly appear.)*

What happens when the base is applied to the paper and then covered with the acid? *(The deep red-orange lines disappear.)*

Why did the paper react to the soap and not to the vinegar or lemon juice? *(The dye used in the paper contains a substance that reacts chemically only to bases.)*

Explaining the Phenomenon

Some substances are called *acids*. Sour foods contain acids, such as vinegar or the citric acid in lemons, oranges, and other fruits. Other substances are called *bases*. Some common examples of bases are soaps, ammonia, and baking soda.

Certain substances known as *indicators* have the property of changing color in the presence of an acid or a base. There are many different kinds of indicators. The dye in the goldenrod paper contains an indicator that turns a deep red-orange color in the presence of a base, like soap.

When you added lemon juice or vinegar to the soap on the paper, the deep red-orange color slowly faded. This happened because lemon juice and vinegar are acids. As you added more acid to the base, the acid began to *neutralize* the base. In other words, the addition of the acid made the soap less and less basic, or alkaline. Finally, you reached a point where the soap had no effect at all on the color of the goldenrod paper. This was the point of neutralization. Enough acid had been added until the substance was no longer a base; it had been neutralized by the acid.

note

For a more detailed explanation of acids and bases, see "Acids and Bases: Background Information" on page 98.

Creating

1. Tell students that they will use the effects created by bases and acids on goldenrod paper to create a design using both positive and negative shapes.

2. Demonstrate the procedure:

Use a moistened piece of bar soap to draw several lines across a sheet of goldenrod paper. Explain that the red-orange lines form a *positive shape,* while the background forms a *negative shape.*

Next, use the bar soap to draw a solid shape approximately 2" x 3". Point out that this is another positive shape.

Dip a bristle brush into lemon juice or vinegar and paint a smaller shape inside the solid shape drawn with the soap. As the acid neutralizes the base, the smaller shape will appear. As you work, explain that you are drawing a negative shape within the positive shape.

Continue to draw positive shapes with the soap. Use the acid to draw negative shapes inside the positive shapes. Explain that both positive and negative shapes interact to form a unified design.

Use crayons to add positive shapes in different colors to the overall design.

3. Tell students to fill an entire sheet of goldenrod paper with positive and negative shapes. Some positive shapes should have negative shapes inside them, and vice versa.

4. When students understand the procedure, distribute the materials and have them begin. Circulate, and offer assistance as needed.

Evaluating

Display the finished designs for everyone to see. Ask students to identify the interaction of positive and negative shapes in their own designs and in the designs of their classmates.

Going Further

Have students generate a list of questions for further investigation. Examples of such questions are:

- *What other substances are bases?* Students can test a range of substances, using the goldenrod paper as an indicator. Obtain such substances as salad oil, tomato juice, grapefruit juice, ammonia, liquid antacid medications, baking soda, and so on. Have students record their results in a journal or logbook.

- *What other substances are indicators?* Students can obtain indicators from a variety of natural substances. Soaking red cabbage leaves in hot water will yield a deep purple indicator that will turn green in the presence of a base and red in the presence of an acid. Dark cherries, when crushed, yield an indicator for both bases and acids. Both purple violets and blue iris petals, when soaked in hot water, yield an indicator for both bases and acids as well. Students can soak white paper in the resulting solutions and then test the paper using lemon juice and baking soda solution. Have them record their results in a journal or logbook.

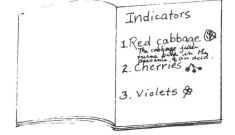

Additional Resources

Alexander, Kay. "Paper Cutouts," in *Learning to Look and Create: The Spectra Program, Grade Four.* Palo Alto, Calif.: Dale Seymour, 1988.

Mullin, Virginia L. *Chemistry Experiments for Children.* New York: Dover, 1962.

● ●

Acids and Bases: Background Information

An individual atom is bound together by the attraction of its positive nucleus for the negative electrons surrounding it. Certain atoms, however, may tend to lose one or more of their outermost electrons. Hydrogen, sodium, and potassium atoms tend to lose one electron each; calcium, magnesium, and copper atoms tend to part with two electrons; and the aluminum atom may release three. On the other hand, certain other atoms tend to gain additional electrons rather than losing some they already possess. Chlorine, bromine, and iodine atoms tend to gain one electron each, while oxygen and sulfur atoms may gain two.

An atom that has gained or lost one or more electrons is no longer a neutrally charged atom. An atom that has more than its normal number of negative electrons is negatively charged and is called a *negative ion.* One which has lost electrons has positive charge and is called a *positive ion.*

An *acid* is a substance containing hydrogen ions (H+). An acid donates hydrogen ions in a reaction. Acids taste sour and are usually very corrosive. Examples of acids include hydrochloric acid (HCl), carbonic acid, or soda water (H_2CO_3), acetic acid, or vinegar (CH_3COOH), and acetylsalicylic acid, or aspirin ($CH_3COOC_6H_4COOH$).

A *base* is a substance containing hydroxyl ions, (OH–). A base accepts hydrogen ions in a chemical reaction. Bases taste bitter and are usually corrosive. Examples of bases include ammonium hydroxide, or ammonia water (NH_4OH), and calcium hydroxide, or limewater ($Ca(OH)_2$) .

A *salt* forms when an acid and a base react with one another. A salt is an ionic compound formed after the free hydrogen ions have detached themselves from the acid and the free hydroxyl ions have detached themselves from the base. Examples of salts are sodium chloride, or table salt (NaCl), and magnesium sulfate, or Epsom salts ($MgSO_4$).

Acid Rain

Overview

What is acid rain? Why is it so damaging to buildings, ancient ruins, and outdoor sculptures? Students discover the answers to these questions as they create minisculptures from limestone (antidust chalk), immerse them in a simulation of acid rain (vinegar), and observe the results.

Student Objectives

■ observe that the interaction of vinegar (acetic acid) and calcium carbonate is a chemical reaction.

■ carve small sculptures from chalk.

Materials

■ safety goggles

■ jumbo paper clips

■ antidust chalk (have extra pieces available in case of breakage)

■ water

■ small plastic cups, 2 per student and 2 for the teacher

■ Logsheet 21: Acid Rain (page 182)

■ white vinegar

■ newspapers to cover work areas

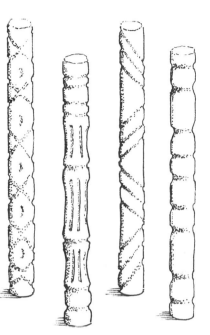

note
Students should be organized into pairs.

SAFETY TIP

In accordance with your school safety policy, make safety goggles available for your students and have students wear them when using acids. Remind students not to taste chemicals or bring them into contact with their eyes or skin and to wash their hands thoroughly after completing the activity. Vinegar is an irritant to the eyes but is otherwise safe to use.

Getting Ready

1. Make sure the chalk you will be using is antidust chalk. Antidust chalk is made from limestone (calcium carbonate.) Ordinary chalk is made from gypsum (calcium sulfate).

2. For each pair of students, prepare two cups. Pour one inch of vinegar into the first cup and one inch of water into the second. Organize the cups, chalk, paper clips, and logsheets for easy distribution during the lesson.

3. Cover work areas with newspaper.

Observing, Comparing, and Describing

1. Begin by having students share their knowledge of acid rain. The following questions are useful in guiding discussion:

What is acid rain? *(Rain containing such acids as sulfuric, sulfurous, nitric, and carbonic acids)*

Why does it do so much damage to buildings and outdoor sculptures? *(Acids react with the calcium carbonate in marble and limestone, causing the rock to disintegrate.)*

2. Explain that materials like marble and limestone are often used in buildings and sculptures. Both marble and limestone contain a mineral called calcium carbonate, which can be written as $CaCO_3$.

3. Tell students that they will conduct an experiment to learn about the effects of acid rain. First, they will create their own minisculptures from calcium carbonate. Next, they will drop a liquid similar to acid rain over them and observe the result.

Creating

1. Demonstrate the procedure:

Straighten one end of a jumbo paper clip.

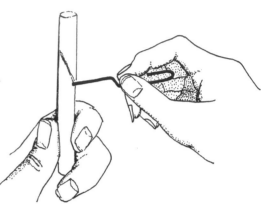

Dip a piece of chalk into a cup of water until the entire surface is wet.

Use the straight end of the clip to score lines in the wet chalk. To make deep lines in the chalk, gently score over existing lines several times rather than applying pressure. (Too much pressure can break the chalk.)

2. Ask students what sorts of designs you could carve in the chalk by using the clip. Explain that the finished sculpture should be as detailed as possible. The entire surface of the chalk should be covered with designs.

3. When students understand the procedure, distribute chalk, paper clips, and water. Circulate as students create their designs, and offer assistance as needed.

Observing, Comparing, and Describing

1. Ask students to predict what will happen to their chalk when it is placed in water and what will happen when it is placed in vinegar. Record the predictions on the chalkboard.

2. Distribute copies of Logsheet 21: Acid Rain. Tell students that as they each complete the logsheet, they should share ideas and observations with their partner.

3. Demonstrate the procedure:

Put on safety goggles and place your piece of chalk upright in a cup of water and observe what happens for several minutes. Write your observations on the logsheet.

Next, place the dry end of the chalk upright in a cup of vinegar. Observe what happens, and record your observations.

4. When students understand the procedure, distribute the safety goggles and the cups of water and vinegar, and have them begin. Circulate, and offer assistance as needed.

Drawing Conclusions

Have students share their observations. The following questions are useful in guiding discussion:

How did the chalk interact with the water? *(No observable reaction)*

How did the chalk interact with the vinegar? *(Bubbles formed, and beige sludge appeared in the bottom of the cup.)*

Any difference in the two ends of chalk at the end of the experiment? *(Very little difference—more exposure to acetic acid would be required to obliterate the carvings.)*

What can we conclude about the effect of acid rain on buildings and sculptures made of limestone or marble? *(Over a period of time, such buildings and sculptures would sustain damage.)*

Explaining the Phenomenon

When you place chalk in vinegar, a chemical reaction occurs between the chalk, $CaCO_3$ (calcium carbonate), and the vinegar, CH_3COOH (acetic acid).

Each molecule of calcium carbonate joins with two molecules of acetic acid to form calcium acetate and carbon dioxide. The chemical equation is expressed below.

$$CaCO_3 + 2CH_3 COOH \rightarrow Ca(CH_3COO)_2 \bullet H_2O + CO_2\uparrow$$

Carbon dioxide gas appears as small bubbles that form when the acetic acid is poured on the chalk. The calcium acetate appears as the light beige sludge that collects in the bottom of the plastic cup.

Going Further

Have students generate a list of questions for further investigation. Examples of such questions are:

■ *How acidic is our local water?* Students can collect such local water samples as tap water, rain water, pond water, and so on. They then can test each sample with pH paper and compare the results. Normal rain in some areas such as the Great Plains and coastal regions may have a pH as high as 6 or 7. If your sample has a pH lower than 5.0, it is considered to be acid rain. Many newspapers include an acid rain report in their weather sections. If such reports are available, students can compare their pH readings with those published in the newspaper. Have students record their observations in a journal or logbook.

■ *What areas of the world are most affected by acid rain?* Students can practice their geography skills by using a world map and resource books to locate the geographical regions most severely affected by acid rain. Such geographical regions would include the former East Germany, Poland, the northeastern

note

Students may wonder whether acid rain is more or less acidic than vinegar, which was used in the experiment to simulate acid rain. Explain that vinegar has a pH of about 4.5. Pure water has a pH of 7. pH values less than 7.0 are considered to be acidic; those greater than 7.0 are basic. Some acid rain samples from certain areas have a measured pH value of 3 or lower.

note

Teachers of younger students may wish to omit the chemical formulas and the equation from this part of the lesson.

note

See "Acid Rain: Background Information" on page 102 for more information.

region of the United States, Great Britain, Japan, Norway, Sweden, and other countries.

- *How does acid rain affect the growth and development of plants?* Students can design an experiment to test the effects of acid rain on the growth and development of plants. For example, students may plant experimental and control groups of radishes. Have them water the control group with plain water and the experimental group with vinegar and graph the results.

Additional Resources

Gay, Kathlyn. *Acid Rain.* New York: Watts, 1983.

Miller, Christina G. and Louise A. Berry. *Acid Rain.* New York: Julian Messner, 1986.

"Precipitation Reactions," in *Chemical Education for Public Understanding Program: Toxic Waste: A Teaching Simulation,* University of California at Berkeley. Menlo Park, Calif.: Addison-Wesley, 1991.

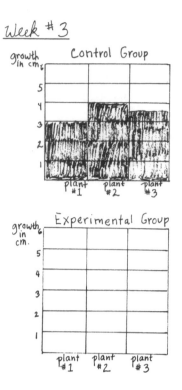

• •

Acid Rain: Background Information

Many people regard acid rain as one of the most serious environmental problems of our time. In the Adirondack mountains, rain has become so acidic that it damages trees and lakes. Acid rain destroys plant and animal life in streams, damages forests, and erodes buildings and other outdoor structures. The effects of acid rain have been observed in other areas of the United States, as well as in Europe, Russia, Canada, Japan, and other countries.

Rain is naturally somewhat acidic. Lightning produces such atmospheric gases as nitrogen oxide, and volcanoes produce such gases as sulfur dioxide. These gases dissolve in rain drops to produce dilute solutions of various acids.

During the 20th century, the acidity of rain increased because of pollution. Factories and automobiles spew nitrogen oxides and sulfur dioxide into the air during the manufacturing process. Sulfur dioxide reacts chemically with water to form sulfuric and sulfurous acids, and nitrogen oxides react with water to form nitric acid.

The World Resources Institute reported that along the Appalachian Mountain chain, rain is 10 times more acidic than nearby lower elevations and about 100 times greater than unpolluted rain. The most acidic rain measured at several eastern mountains is 2000 times worse than unpolluted water. In fact, it is so acidic that it approximates lemon juice.

Many of the world's ancient monuments and structures, such as the Egyptian pyramids, the Roman Colosseum, and the Gothic churches of Europe are showing signs of damage caused by acid rain. In Washington, DC, the marble of the Capitol Building, the Washington Monument, and the Lincoln Memorial may be suffering damage from acid rain.

Garbage Sculptures

Overview

In this activity, the teacher challenges students to pick up as much outdoor litter as they can in 15 minutes. Students work outdoors in groups of four, categorizing and recording the number of trash items they pick up. Then, after a class discussion about the interaction of litter and the environment, students recycle clean trash items they have brought from home by using them to create bas-relief sculptures.

Student Objectives

- identify a wide variety of trash items found on the schoolyard and observe which can be recycled.

- create a bas-relief sculpture with clean throwaway objects brought from home.

- create a design using the elements of repetition and texture.

Materials

- large trash bags for collecting litter on the schoolyard, 1 per group of 4 students

- thick gloves, 1 pair per student

- Logsheet 22: Outdoor Trash (page 183), 1 per group of four students

- assorted clean throwaway objects, such as scraps of cardboard, toilet paper tubes, paper towel tubes, paper cups, egg cartons, bottle caps, buttons, scraps of aluminum foil, metal and plastic lids, twists and bread ties, knobs, and wire.

- white glue

- shallow containers for glue and for water, such as cut-off milk cartons

- newspapers to cover work areas

- sheets of stiff tagboard, 9" x 12"

- stiff-bristle brushes, 1" wide

- tempera paint in assorted colors

Getting Ready

1. Select an area of the school for the cleanup activity.

2. Have your students begin collecting and cleaning various throwaway objects before you start the lesson. These can be brought from home.

SAFETY TIP

Tell students to avoid collecting breakable objects or objects with sharp edges.

3. Pour white glue into several shallow containers, one per group of four students. Fill several containers with water. Cover work areas with newspaper.

4. Organize collections of objects into shallow tubs or bags for easy distribution during the lesson, along with the tagboard, stiff-bristle brushes, and glue.

5. Set aside an area of the classroom where the finished sculptures can dry undisturbed.

Note
Students should be organized into groups of four.

Observing, Comparing, and Describing

1. Begin by having students share what they know about litter and recycling. The following questions are useful in guiding discussion:

What is litter? *(Trash lying scattered about)*

What kinds of things do we throw away? *(Paper, plastic, metal, glass, food scraps, etc.)*

Why is litter harmful? *(It causes pollution; it takes up space in landfills; animals sometimes choke on plastic objects.)*

What is recycling? *(Reusing items that otherwise would be thrown away)*

What kinds of things can be recycled? *(Newspaper, cans, glass and plastic bottles, etc.)*

2. Ask students to list the different kinds of litter they might find outside on the schoolyard (or in some other designated area). List these on the chalkboard.

3. Discuss how the materials listed on the chalkboard could be categorized. For example, gum wrappers and paper cups could be grouped in a category called *paper*. List the categories on the chalkboard.

4. Combine the categories into the following: paper, plastic, metal, glass, food, and other. Ask students to predict which category will make up the largest amount of outdoor litter, which will make up the next largest, and so on.

5. Tell students that they will be working in groups of four to pick up as much litter as they can in 15 minutes. Each group will be given a large trash bag to hold the litter and heavy gloves to wear.

6. Distribute one copy of Logsheet 22: Outdoor Trash to each group of students. Explain that each litter item the group picks up must be recorded on the logsheet with a tally mark. Have each group select a member to be the recorder.

7. When students understand the procedure, distribute gloves, a trash bag, a logsheet, and a pencil to each group, and take the class outdoors to begin the cleanup activity. After 15 minutes, signal the groups to stop collecting.

8. Have students deposit the trash bags in the school trash receptacle. Then take the class back indoors.

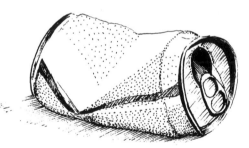

SAFETY TIP
Direct your students to wear heavy gloves to protect their hands from sharp objects.

9. Tell students to total their tally marks for each category. Next, have them graph the totals on the logsheet.

Drawing Conclusions

1. Have a member from each group report the number of trash items collected in each category. Write these numbers on the chalkboard under the category headings.

2. Ask students to calculate the class total for the amounts listed under each category heading. Have students compare these amounts with their earlier predictions.

3. Help students speculate about the causes and problems of litter. The following questions are useful in guiding discussion:

Who do you think is responsible for the litter you found? *(We are.)*

How does the litter affect this environment? *(Much of the trash found outside decays very slowly, if at all, and provides no useful nutrients for plants. Plastic is especially long-lasting. A plastic six-pack beverage holder is dangerous to wildlife— many animals choke to death when their heads catch in the plastic loops.)*

When we throw these litter-filled trash bags away, where will they go? *(Probably to a local landfill site or to an incinerator)*

What suggestions do you have for reducing the amount of litter in this area? *(Reduce the amount of packaging so there is less waste; pick up and recycle, etc.)*

Explaining the Phenomenon

The following table shows an estimate of the different kinds and percentages of trash items Americans throw away each day.

Item	% of Daily Waste
Paper	36%
Yard	20%
Food	9%
Metals	9%
Glass	8%
Plastics	7%
Textiles	6%
Rubber & Leather	3%
Miscellaneous	2%

Source: *Garbage!* by Evan and Janet Hadingham. New York: Simon & Schuster, 1990.

The United States Environmental Protection Agency (EPA) has developed a *waste hierarchy*. Explain that a *hierarchy* is a classification or organization arranged in order of importance or priority. The EPA's waste hierarchy places most importance on reducing waste at its source. The next most important means of waste reduction is recycling, followed by incineration and the use of landfills.

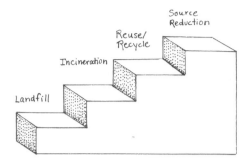

The first two categories in the waste hierarchy are strategies that we can all use at home. *Source reduction* involves generating less waste at home. Examples include taking shorter showers, using reusable lunch boxes instead of paper bags, and so on. Many objects can be *recycled*, or used again (paper, aluminum, glass, certain plastics, etc.).

Creating

1. Explain that finding alternative uses for things is one way of recycling. For example, when an artist uses trash items to create a sculpture, he or she is recycling the trash into a work of art.

2. Tell students that they will create a bas-relief sculpture using clean throwaway objects. Explain that *bas-relief* is a sculpture in which the forms project only slightly from the surface.

3. Demonstrate the procedure: First, show students a piece of tagboard, and explain that it will serve as the surface for the bas-relief. Arrange a variety of throwaway objects on the tagboard to create an interesting pattern or design. As you work, help students notice how the objects project from the surface. Have them notice examples of repetition in your design. Point out the various textures created by the objects.

4. Tell students that they should experiment with several designs until they are ready to make a final design with glue.

5. Dip a stiff bristle brush into a container of glue. Using broad, horizontal strokes, cover the surface of the tagboard with a thick layer of glue. Wipe excess glue against the edge of the container, and place the brush, bristles down, into a container of water.

6. Next, arrange the objects in a design on the glue surface. Press each object firmly into the glue.

7. When students understand the procedure, distribute tagboard and collections of clean throwaway objects. *Do not distribute the glue at this time.* Allow sufficient time for students to experiment with a variety of designs on the tagboard. Circulate, and offer assistance when needed.

8. When students are ready to create their final designs, distribute the containers of glue, brushes, and water. Encourage students to paint the glue on thickly. Remind them to place their brushes in the water when they have finished with the glue.

Final Touches

1. When the bas-relief sculptures have dried, have students paint them with tempera paint. Students may choose to paint their sculptures just one color or several.

Note

For more information, see "Garbage: Background Information" on page 108.

2. Mount the sculptures against a black construction paper background for an attractive bulletin board display.

Evaluating

Display the finished sculptures. Ask students to look for examples of repetition in the bas-reliefs. Help them notice and compare the textures created by various kinds of objects.

Going Further

Have students generate a list of questions for further investigation. Examples of such questions are:

- *What kinds of litter are biodegradable?* Have students cut large milk cartons to make planters. Fill each carton with soil. Collect one each of the following: scrap of aluminum foil, piece of string, piece of banana, tin can, plastic wrapper, green leaf. Bury one item in each milk carton planter. Keep the soil warm and damp. Once a week, over an 8-week period, have students unearth the items and record the appearance. At the end of the 8-week period, empty the containers and have students notice which items have decayed—these are the biodegradable ones.

- *What kinds of packaging are used in a grocery store?* Students can conduct a research investigation at their local grocery store to try to identify the different materials (plastic, aluminum, paper, etc.) used in packaging. They can speculate as to the main purpose of each packaging item—whether it was to keep food fresh, to protect the product from damage during shipping, to attract consumers, and so on. They can also identify any items they consider to be examples of overpackaging and suggest ways that some items might be alternatively packaged.

- *How much garbage does one family throw away in one day?* Have students survey the items that are thrown away at home. Follow up the survey with a class discussion in which students speculate about ways to reduce the amount of trash we discard daily.

Additional Resources

Bailey, Donna. *What We Can Do about Recycling Garbage.* New York: Watts, 1991.

Hadingham, Evan and Janet. *Garbage!* New York: Simon & Schuster, 1990.

Simons, Robin. *Recyclopedia.* Boston: Houghton Mifflin, 1976.

"The Waste Hierarchy: Where is 'Away'?" in *Chemical Education for Public Understanding Program.* University of California at Berkeley. Menlo Park, Calif.: Addison-Wesley, 1993.

• •

Garbage: Background Information

By some estimates, the average American today throws away 3.5 pounds of municipal solid waste each day, or nearly 1,300 pounds per year. Much of our garbage ends up in already overcrowded municipal landfills. A *landfill* is simply a large hole in the ground where garbage is covered with soil. Many landfills contain such hazardous products as household cleaners, paints, oils, and fertilizers. The chemicals from such products can mix with rainwater and trickle down to contaminate a town's drinking water.

Some trash is taken to *incinerators,* which are gargbage-burning plants. Burning eliminates a huge volume of garbage because at least three-quarters of it goes up in smoke. Another advantage is that many new incinerators are designed to produce energy from burning garbage. However, incinerators are extremely expensive to build and may pose a serious health risk because burning trash can send chemicals up the smokestack and into the atmosphere.

Recycling, or reusing products and materials, can be a more economical alternative to either incineration or landfilling. For example, making new aluminum cans from old ones is much less expensive than making them from raw materials. As a result, there is a strong demand for recycled cans. In 1988 over half the cans sold in America were collected for reprocessing into new cans. However, not all trash items are currently recycled. Only a tiny fraction of plastic containers are recycled, and old plastic cannot be recycled it if contains dirt or such contaminants as glue, paper labels, or bottle caps.

The most effective way to reduce the amount of garbage we throw away each day is *source reduction*—generating less waste at the home, office, and factory. We can generate less waste through such means as using less paper, reusing paper shopping bags, using recycled paper, reusing plastic bags, plastic picnic plates and utensils, making a compost pile with yard wastes, and so on.

Animal Adaptations

Overview

How are animals adapted for seeing, sensing, eating, hiding, and defending themselves? In this activity, students compare a variety of animals and observe the ways in which the animals are adapted for obtaining food and protection. They then invent their own imaginary animals and sculpt them out of papier-mâché.

Student Objectives

- observe that animals have adaptations that enable them to obtain food and to protect themselves from enemies.

- create a fantasy animal sculpture out of papier-mâché.

Materials

- masking tape
- Logsheet 23: Animal Adaptations (page 184)
- pictures of a variety animals, from magazines, posters, or photographs
- newspapers
- shallow containers, such as aluminum pie pans, cut-off milk cartons, etc.
- liquid starch
- materials for decorating, such as tagboard pieces, toothpicks, yarn, and pipe cleaners
- scissors
- white glue
- tempera paint, assorted colors
- brushes
- water
- (optional) clear varnish

Getting Ready

1. Collect magazines or posters with pictures of animals. Students can bring magazines from home to add to the collection. You will need at least two pictures for each group of four students. Organize magazines and logsheets for easy distribution during the "Observing, Comparing, and Describing" portion of the lesson.

2. Organize art materials for distribution during the "Creating" portion of the lesson. Each group of four students will need newspapers, masking tape, two shallow containers of liquid starch, scissors, glue, and such decorating materials as toothpicks, tagboard pieces, yarn, and pipe cleaners.

3. Cover work areas with newspaper.

4. Set aside an area of the classroom where finished sculptures can dry undisturbed.

5. For a later session, after the sculptures have dried, organize containers of tempera paint, brushes, and water for distribution to groups of students.

note

Students should be organized into groups of four.

note

The art activity will require at least two sessions: the first to create the papier-mâché sculptures, and the second to paint them after they have dried.

Observing, Comparing, and Describing

1. Begin by having students share their knowledge of various adaptations. The following questions are useful in guiding discussion:

   How do some animals sense their environment? *(By smelling, seeing, hearing, feeling)*

   How do some animals move? *(By crawling, sliding, creeping, climbing, running, etc.)*

   How do some animals defend themselves? *(Claws, teeth, spines, poison, etc.)*

   How do some animals hide from their enemies? *(By camouflage, in holes, by remaining motionless, etc.)*

2. Tell students that every animal species is *adapted*, or formed, for seeing, sensing, eating, hiding, and defending itself. An *adaptation* is a change in a species that fits it better for its environment.

3. Humans have many adaptations. For example, our opposable thumbs enable us to grasp tools. To show how useful this adaptation is, ask several volunteers to come to the front of the class. Tape their thumbs to their hands with masking tape. Have them try to pick things up, to write on the chalkboard, and to tie their shoes or button their shirts.

4. Show students a picture of an animal, and ask them to notice how it is adapted for seeing, sensing, eating, hiding, and defending itself. List student responses on the chalkboard.

5. Show students a picture of a second animal, and ask them to notice how it adapted for seeing, sensing, eating, hiding, and defending itself.

6. Have students compare the adaptations of the two animals. The following questions are useful for guiding discussion:

   What are the similarities and differences in the way these two animals might see and sense their environment?

   What are the similarities and differences in the way these two animals might eat? How might their adaptations affect what they can and cannot eat?

Where might each of these animals hide? In what kind of environment would each animal be most noticeable?

What are the similarities and differences in the way these two animals might defend themselves? Are their defensive adaptations more suitable for fighting or hiding?

7. Tell students that they will work in groups of four to compare the adaptations of two different animals. Distribute copies of Logsheet 23: Animal Adaptations. Tell students that as they complete the logsheet, each person should share ideas and observations with others in the group.

8. When students understand the procedure, distribute two different animal pictures to each group and have them begin Circulate, and offer assistance as needed.

Drawing Conclusions

Have each group share its list of animal adaptations. Help students speculate about how each adaptation better fits the animal for its environment.

Explaining the Phenomenon

A *species* is a group of individuals that have attributes in common and can breed with one another. For example, a bald eagle is a species of bird.

As a species changes to better fit a new environment, its changes affect that environment, causing still more environmental changes. The species must then change again, thereby causing the environment to change further, and so on.

note

For more information about the interaction between an animal and its environment in the process of adaptation, see "Adaptation: Background Information" on page 113.

Creating

1. Tell students that they will create a sculpture of a fantasy animal using papier-mâché. Explain that *papier-mâché* is an art material made of paper that has been torn into strips or pulp and covered with a paste or glue mixture. It can be shaped into different forms when wet and is solid and very hard when dry.

2. Explain that their fantasy creature must have imaginary adaptations for seeing, sensing, eating, and defending itself. Its coloration must serve either to camouflage it in the classroom environment or to be conspicuous. Help students brainstorm a variety of possible creatures. Allow time for sharing.

3. Demonstrate the procedure:

First, create a skeleton for the creature you want to make. Use rolls of newspaper to make the body, legs, and head, as shown. The rolls can be held together with masking tape.

After the skeleton is completed, adjust the position of the animal. Tape wads of crumpled paper to parts of the body to make them appear thicker or fatter.

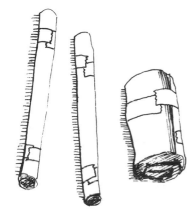

Tear newspaper into strips approximately 1/2" x 3" long. Dip them one at a time into liquid starch, wetting both sides. Lay each strip onto the creature and wrap it tightly around body contours. Position each strip so that it overlaps the others.

Cover the creature's entire body, adding only one layer at a time, until the creature is shaped in the desired form.

Add final details, such as large ears, fins, or tails, by attaching pieces of tagboard to the body with strips of papier-mâché, as shown. Toothpicks can be glued to the body to represent spines. Pipe cleaners can be attached to represent antennae, and so on.

4. When students understand the procedure, distribute the materials and allow them to begin. Circulate, and offer assistance as needed.

5. After the creatures are completed, have students set them aside in a designated area to dry for several days.

6. When papier-mâché is dry, it becomes strong and hard and is ready to be painted. Have students think about the kind of coloration their creature will have. Will it be camouflaged against a certain kind of background (cryptic coloration), or will it be bright and conspicuous (warning coloration)? Have students paint their creatures with tempera paints.

Final Touches

The finished papier-mâché sculptures may be covered with a clear varnish or shellac to give them a glossy shine.

Evaluating

Display the finished animals. Have students notice and compare the different adaptations created by their peers. Allow students to talk about how their animals are adapted for survival.

Going Further

Have students generate a list of questions for further investigation. Examples of such questions are :

- *How are other animals adapted for obtaining food?* Bring in pictures of different kinds of animals, and have students discuss the types of food each eats and whether each animal has a physical characteristic adapted for catching and eating the food. For instance, the long neck of a giraffe enables it to eat tree leaves.

- *How do organisms adapt over time?* Play a simulation game that illustrates change in animals in terms of camouflage characteristics. Obtain a box of colored cereal with a variety of colored pieces, some brightly colored, and others tan or beige. Scatter several handfuls over an area of dirt approximately 30' x 30'. Tell students that they are to play the part of birds that will feed on worms in the dirt. At a time signal, let the "birds" collect as many "worms" as they can by picking up one piece of cereal at a time and placing it in an envelope before picking up another piece. After several minutes, return to class and make a histogram of the results.

Additional Resources

Barrett, Norman. *Birds of Prey.* New York: Watts, 1991.

Bender, Lionel. *Fish to Reptiles.* New York: Watts, 1988.

Freedman, Russel. *Tooth and Claw: A Look at Animal Weapons.* New York: Holiday, 1980.

Goor, Ron, and Nancy Goor. *All Kinds of Feet.* New York: Crowell, 1984.

Lowery, Lawrence F. "Ecology," in *The Everyday Science Sourcebook.* Palo Alto, Calif.: Dale Seymour, 1985.

• •

Adaptation: Background Information

In our world, lands and seas and climates continually change. When an organism finds itself in a changed environment, it too must change or die. The change in a species to better fit its environment is called *adaptation*.

Adaptation is a never-ending interaction between organisms and the selecting power of the environment. As organisms change to better fit a changed environment, their changes impact the environment, causing still more environmental changes. The organisms may then change again, thereby causing the environment to change further, and so on.

Adaptive change occurs as the result of variation within a species and the selecting power of the environment. An example of plant adaptation is the interaction between plants and a dry, rocky terrain. As some generations of plants adapted to a desert environment, they acted on the soil to make it deeper and better able to hold scarce water. As a result, subsequent generations had to adapt further to survive in less dry soil conditions.

An example of animal adaptation is the development of *protective coloration,* or camouflage, in the British peppered moth, *Biston betularia.* Prior to 1850, most of the moths were light-colored. Over the next 50 years or so, increasing numbers of dark-colored ones were collected. Eventually the dark forms came to comprise almost the entire population of moths in areas where factory smoke darkened the trunks of nearby trees. Birds could easily find and catch the light-colored moths because they stood out against the darkened tree trunks, whereas dark-colored moths against dark backgrounds were difficult to find. As a result, the numbers of light-colored moths dwindled and the numbers of dark-colored moths increased.

Seed Adaptations

Overview

How do seeds travel? In this autumn activity, students go outdoors to collect different seeds for observation and classification. They notice that some seed species have become adapted to float through the air, while others fall to the ground or stick to animals. Then, using a variety of materials, they create their own imaginary seeds with adaptations for travel.

Student Objectives

- observe that seeds are adapted to disperse in a variety of ways.

- classify seeds according to whether they disperse by floating through the air, falling to the ground, or sticking to animals.

- use a variety of materials to sculpt an imaginary seed.

Materials

- newspapers to cover work areas

- bags or other small containers for carrying seeds

- Logsheet 24: Seed Classification (page 185), 1 per group of 4 students

- assorted materials for creating imaginary seeds: modeling clay, tape, toothpicks, string, paper clips, pipe cleaners, construction paper, bits of plastic foam, yarn, tissue paper, etc.

- clear tape, 1 roll per group of students

Getting Ready

1. Cover work areas with newspaper.

2. Organize collection bags, logsheets, tape, and art materials for easy distribution during the lesson.

3. Select a weedy area outdoors for seed collection.

Observing, Comparing, and Describing

1. Begin by having students share their knowledge of seeds. The following questions are useful in guiding discussion:

What is a seed? *(A plant part containing an embryo, capable of germination to produce a new plant.)*

Where are seeds found? *(Inside fruits, on or near plants)*

Why do plants have seeds? *(To reproduce)*

note

Students should be organized into groups of four.

SAFETY TIP

Students with severe allergies should not venture into the weedy area to collect seeds. They can assist their group to classify the seeds indoors once the seeds have been collected.

How are seeds different/similar? *(Show several varieties to students.) (Size, shape, color, etc.)*

How do plants spread, or travel, to different areas? *(Fall or are picked up and carried by wind, water, or animals)*

2. Help students understand that seed species are adapted, or formed, for travel. Without travel, seeds would fall directly under the parent plant. The area soon would become so overcrowded that the young plants could not survive.

3. Explain that some seeds, like those of the dandelion, float through the air. Others are hitchhikers that travel by sticking to the fur or feathers of animals. Some fall to the ground, and others are carried by water.

4. Tell students that they will be working in groups of four to collect as many different kinds of seeds as possible. They should look for seeds that float, fall, or stick.

5. Distribute bags or other containers for collecting, and take students outdoors to collect seeds.

6. After groups have finished collecting, bring the students indoors, and have them sit at their desks or tables. Ask them to remove the seeds from their bags and to categorize them into three groups. In one pile, place all of the seeds that *float* through the air, such as dandelion, milkweed, and thistle. In another pile, place seeds that *fall* to the ground. In a third pile, place seeds that *stick* to things, such as foxtail and cocklebur. (They may find some of these on their socks!)

7. Distribute one copy of Logsheet 24: Seed Classification to each group of students. Have students select a member of the group to record information on the logsheet.

8. Tell students to tape their group's seeds onto the appropriate areas of the logsheet. Then, have them count each kind of seed they collected and graph the information on the logsheet.

Drawing Conclusions

Tell students to examine the seeds after they have been classified and counted. The following questions are useful in guiding discussion:

How many of each kind of seed did your group collect? *(Answers will vary.)*

How are the seeds that float through the air similar or different? How does their structure help them float on air currents?

How would you describe the seeds that fall to the ground?

How are the seeds that stick similar or different? How does their structure help them stick?

What seeds don't seem to fit in any of these groups? How would you describe them?

note

Most seeds are quite small and low to the ground, so advise students to look carefully to find them.

float

fall

stick

Explaining the Phenomenon

In our world, lands and seas and climates continually change. When a plant species finds itself in a changed environment, it too must change, or die. The change in a plant species to better fit its environment is called *adaptation*.

It is the species, not the individual, that adapts. A *species* is a group of individuals having attributes in common and the ability to interbreed. For example, a dandelion is a species of plant. Adaptation occurs as the result of variation within a species and the selecting power of the environment.

An example of plant adaptation is the interaction between plants and a dry, rocky terrain. As some plants adapted to a desert environment, they acted on the soil to make it deeper and better able to hold scarce water. As a result, they then had to adapt further to survive in less dry soil conditions.

note

For more information, see "Adaptation: Background Information" on page 113.

Creating

1. Tell students that they next will create their own imaginary seed. Their seed must be adapted to travel in some way.

2. Explain the procedure:

Look over a variety of materials (such as those listed in the "Materials" section at the beginning of the lesson). Decide whether to make a seed that can float, fall to the ground, or stick.

Use as many types of materials as possible in order to make your seed look unique.

3. When students understand the procedure, distribute materials and have them begin. Circulate, and offer assistance as needed.

Evaluating

Display the finished sculptures. Have students compare and discuss the variety of ways their classmates created seeds that can float, fall, or stick.

Going Further

Have students generate a list of questions for further investigation. Examples of such questions are:

- *How do flowers produce seeds?* Obtain mature blossoms of thistle and dandelion. Place them in the classroom so that students can observe them dry and go to seed. Find branches of Scotch broom or other plants that still carry seed pods, and bring them to class. Let the branches dry. Have students observe and record the changes in the seed pods. Ask them to listen and watch for signs of seed dispersal. They can record their observations in a journal or logbook.

- *How does the environment affect the germination of seeds?* Students can experiment to discover the effect of water, light, and

temperature on germination. Have students plant equal
amounts of bean seeds in wet and dry soil, keeping all other
conditions the same. Students also can plant equal amounts of
seeds in light and dark conditions and observe the results as the
seeds germinate. Have students freeze a sample of seeds before
planting or bake them in the oven. The growth of the frozen or
baked seeds can be compared with the growth of a control
sample. Students can record their observations in a journal or
logbook.

Additional Resources

Overbeck, Cynthia. *How Seeds Travel.* Minneapolis: Lerner, 1982.

Lauber, Patricia. *Seeds. Pop, Stick, Glide.* New York: Crown, 1981.

The Food Chain

Overview

How does energy flow within a food chain? This investigation begins with a game in which students simulate the interactions of organisms in a food chain. Students assume the roles of animals and try to survive by getting something to eat without being eaten themselves. After playing the game several times, students apply their knowledge by working in cooperative groups to create a food chain mural.

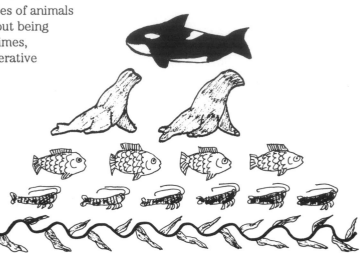

Student Objectives

- observe that the flow of energy within a food chain can result in a balance among various organisms and that a break in the food chain link can destroy the balance.

- work in cooperative groups to create a mural that illustrates the feeding relationships in a food chain.

Materials

- sandwich-sized plastic bags, 1 per student

- pieces of construction paper, approximately 4" x 5", in 3 different colors, each color to represent an animal

- masking tape

- 4–5 qts of popped corn

- whistle or bell to use as a signal

- resource books, such as encyclopedias and books about ecology and animal life, at least 1 per group of 4 students

- colored bulletin board paper, approximately 1 sq yd, 1 per group of 4 students

- white construction paper, 18" x 24"

- pencils

- crayons or colored markers

- scissors

- paste

Getting Ready

1. Select a site for the food chain game. A section of lawn approximately 15–20 yards on a side is sufficient.

2. Spread popped popcorn over the gaming area.

3. Cut pieces of construction paper, approximately 4" x 5", in three different colors, each color to represent an animal. Have enough pieces for 3/4 of the group to be mice, 1/8 to be snakes, and 1/8 to be hawks. Cut one piece of paper for each student.

4. Obtain a collection of resource books about ecology and various kinds of animal life. You will need at least one book per group of four students.

5. For each group of four students, organize a set of materials: colored bulletin board paper (or white butcher paper) approximately one yard square, four sheets of white construction paper, pencils, crayons or colored markers, scissors, and paste.

note
Students should be organized into groups of four.

Observing, Comparing, and Describing

1. Begin by having students share what they know about food chains. Questions to guide discussion are:

What do grasshoppers eat? *(Plants)*

What eats grasshoppers? *(Frogs, birds, etc.)*

What eats the frog or bird that eats grasshoppers? *(Hawks, snakes, etc.)*

2. Draw the relationship on the chalkboard and introduce it as a food chain. Explain that an organism that eats plants is called an herbivore and that an organism that eats animals is called a carnivore. A food chain is a simple model of the sequence of plant-herbivore-carnivore feeding.

3. Ask students to think of other food chains. Examples include:

grass	→	rabbit	→	fox		
grass	→	cow	→	human		
plant	→	beetle	→	spider	→	bird
algae	→	small fish	→	big fish	→	bear

4. Tell students that they will play a game to simulate the feeding relationships in a food chain. Some students will be mice; others will be snakes; others will be hawks. Each student will wear a colored piece of construction paper on his or her back to indicate the animal represented. For example, all the mice might wear yellow squares, the snakes red squares, and the hawks blue squares.

5. Assign an "animal" to each student. Distribute the colored pieces of construction paper along with lengths of masking tape. Have students work with a partner to tape a square to each student's back.

note
You may wish to have students draw the sheets of colored paper from a bag to avoid bickering over who will be which animal.

6. Distribute a plastic bag to each student. Explain that the bags represent stomachs. Students will put their "food" (popcorn) into their "stomachs" (bags) when the game begins.

7. Take students outdoors and show them the gaming area. Explain that the scattered popcorn represents seeds for the mice to eat.

8. Explain the rules of the game:

When the game begins (signaled by the blow of a whistle or sound of a bell), mice must try to collect all the popcorn they can in their "stomachs." At the same time, they must try to avoid being tagged (eaten) by the snakes.

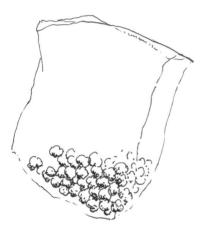

Snakes will try to capture (tag) mice, and hawks will try to capture snakes. When a snake captures a mouse, the mouse's stomach and its contents are emptied into the stomach of the snake. When the hawk captures a snake, he or she simply collects the snake's entire stomach and its contents. Hawks do not eat mice in this game.

Animals that have been captured must turn their food over to their captors. They then must leave the gaming area and sit on the sidelines to watch the rest of the game.

Animals will have five minutes to collect food. For a mouse to survive, it must have filled its stomach bag at least half full. For a snake to survive, it must have filled its stomach to the top (leaving room to close the bag). For a hawk to survive, it must have collected at least two full bags of popcorn.

9. When students understand the procedure, give the signal to play. End the game when either five minutes have elapsed or all of the mice have been eaten. The first time the game is played, it usually lasts only a few seconds, for reasons discussed below.

Drawing Conclusions

1. The following questions are useful in guiding a discussion of the results:

How many animals survived? *(Answers will vary.)*

Was there a balance, with some survivors remaining from each species? *(Probably not)* Why or why not? *(Usually the mice either are eaten before they can forage, or the snakes are eaten and the mice eat their fill unmolested.)*

How could the rules of the game be altered so that there would be a greater balance of survivors after the five-minute day? *(Change the number of mice, snakes, or hawks; let mice return into the game after being eaten; provide a safety zone for mice or snakes; spread out more popcorn, and so on.)*

2. Allow the class to play the game several more times, adding one rule variation for each new game. After each game, have students analyze the results. How many mice ate enough to survive? How many snakes? Hawks?

3. Help students speculate about how the balance of animals at the end of the game compares with balance in the real world. In the balance of nature, there are more plants than plant eaters and more plant eaters than animal eaters. But sometimes this balance can be upset.

The following questions are useful in guiding discussion.

What would happen to the mouse population if there were no snakes? *(It would explode, and the mice would exhaust their food sources and begin to starve.)*

Do the hawks need plants to survive? Why? *(Yes; without plants there would be no mice, and without mice there would be no snakes, the hawks' food source.)*

Do the snakes need the hawks to survive? *(Yes, the snake population would explode and exhaust its food sources without the hawks to keep numbers down through predation.)*

note
For more information about the food chain, see "The Food Chain: Background Information" on page 122.

Creating

1. Tell students that artists sometimes express their ideas in a *mural,* which is a work of art that is applied to the surface of a wall. Explain that students will be working cooperatively in groups to create a mural that illustrates the relationships in a food chain.

2. Have students brainstorm a list of possible food chains and record these on the chalkboard. Explain that as artists, students may choose to represent either actual or imaginary organisms. Point out that if they wish to represent actual organisms, students may use available resource books to gather information about the organisms' appearance and eating habits.

3. Tell students that they will use contrasting elements to create a sense of *balance,* or equilibrium, in the mural. *Contrast* is the use of opposites close together, such as large and small, light and dark, rough and smooth, and so on. One way to use contrast to create a sense of balance is to place shapes of different sizes and quantities in an artwork. For instance, a large drawing of one carnivore can be balanced by several small drawings of herbivores.

4. Explain the procedure:

As a group, decide on a food chain to represent. Use reference books if needed.

Have each group member select an organism to illustrate. One person can draw the carnivore, while others can draw herbivores and plants.

On the colored bulletin board paper, sketch a pencil outline of the largest pyramid shape that can fit on the paper. One large carnivore will be placed at the top of the pyramid, several medium-sized herbivores will be placed in the middle, and many small plants will be placed along the base.

Have each group member first draw a pencil sketch of their organism(s) on a large sheet of white construction paper. Then decide as a group whether to make alterations to the sketches or to color the drawings with markers or crayons.

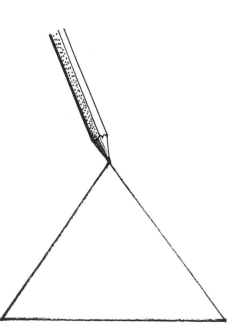

As a group, select colors for each organism. Choose contrasting colors that will create a sense of balance in the mural. Color the pencil drawings with markers or crayons.

Cut out the drawings.

Paste the drawings into place on the pyramid. Place the carnivore on top, the herbivores in the middle, and the plants along the base.

Sign your names in a corner of the mural.

5. Display the finished murals in the classroom or in display areas around the school.

Evaluating

Ask students to compare the murals created by their classmates. The following questions are useful in guiding discussion:

How are the various kinds of food chains similar or different?

How was balance achieved in each mural?

Going Further

Have students generate a list of questions for further investigation. Examples of such questions are:

- *Are the plants in our schoolyard part of a food chain?* Have students go outdoors and look for evidence of plants being used for food. Can they find the animals responsible? Students may record their observations in a journal or logbook.

- *What food chains are humans part of?* Have students keep a record of the foods they eat in a day. They then can list the possible food chains they were a part of for that day. For example, if a student drinks milk with lunch, then he or she is a part of the following food chain:

grass $\rightarrow$ cow $\rightarrow$ human

Additional Resources

Alexander, Kay. "Sculpture in Motion," in *Learning to Look and Create: The Spectra Program, Grade Four.* Palo Alto, Calif.: Dale Seymour, 1988.

"Food Chain Game," in *Outdoor Biology Instructional Strategies.* Berkeley, Calif.: Lawrence Hall of Science, 1975.

• •

The Food Chain: Background Information

All forms of animal life ultimately depend on plant life because animals cannot manufacture their own food. Plants may be eaten by insects or grazing animals or seed-eating birds, which in turn may be eaten by carnivorous animals. Carnivorous animals themselves may then be eaten by still others. A *food chain* is a simple model of the sequence of plant-herbivore-carnivore feeding.

Energy flows within the food chain, from plants, the primary producers, to *herbivores* (plant eaters), and then to *carnivores* (meat eaters). The process may begin in a plant's leaves, where the energy of the sun's light is used to produce sugars, or carbohydrates.

A mouse that eats seeds is obtaining its energy directly from a plant. It is said to be a *first-level consumer,* with the plants as producers. A snake that eats the mouse is a *second-level consumer,* and a hawk that eats the snake is a *third-level consumer.* If a fox should eat the hawk, the fox would be a *fourth-level consumer.*

Feeding patterns in nature are complicated by mixtures of possibilities. For instance, when people eat cereals, they are first-level consumers, but when they eat beef, which fed on grass, they are second-level consumers. Or, a person might eat a fish, which lived on smaller fish, which fed on tiny organisms, which fed on algae, in which case the person is a fourth-level consumer.

A food chain is very simple model of the energy transfer that occurs in nature. In actuality, the transfer is more complex because of the number and variety of organisms involved and the variety of food sources. A more realistic representation might be a *food web,* in which energy and materials may pass through any number of organisms before the energy is finally lost to the system in the form of heat.

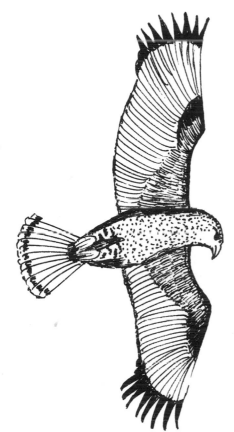

Energy

The Theme of Energy

The investigations in this section are organized around the theme of *energy*. Energy can appear in many forms—as the energy of motion or in the form of heat and light. It can appear in the flow of electrical current or on an atomic or molecular scale as chemical energy. In physics, *energy* is defined as "the ability to do work" or "the ability to make things move." In biology, energy provides living things with the ability to grow and to reproduce. Light, heat, sound, magnetism, and electricity are all manifestations of energy.

Artists use energy in its various forms to create movement or intensity in a work of art. Some sculptural forms, such as mobiles, use wind or heat energy to maintain their motion. Other works of art use the energy produced by neon and laser lights to generate compositions of varied, brightly colored designs.

In the visual arts, *energy* often is expressed metaphorically. Students learn to evoke the quality of energy in their artwork. Bold lines, forceful brush strokes, and bright colors all contribute to vitality of expression in drawing and painting. By learning to evaluate the expressive qualities of their own work, students develop the ability to recognize the quality of energy in the work of other artists.

Energy: Lines of Expression

Overview

What is energy? How can energy be expressed through drawing? The teacher begins this activity by having students brainstorm everything they know about energy. A discussion follows in which students identify energy in its various manifestations: as motion, heat, light, sound, magnetism, chemical and nuclear energy, and electricity. As artists, students then express the quality of energy through gesture drawing.

Student Objectives

- observe that energy is manifested in such forms as motion, heat, light, chemical and nuclear energy, and electricity.

- use charcoal or felt-tip pen to create gesture drawings that express the quality of energy.

Materials

- writing paper, 1 sheet per group of 4 students

- typing or ditto paper, 15 sheets per student

- charcoal or black felt-tip pens

Getting Ready

1. Organize writing paper, typing or ditto paper, and charcoal or pens for distribution during the lesson.

2. Place a sturdy table at the front of the class where everyone can see it. It should be large and stable so that a student can stand safely on top of it.

note

Students should be organized into groups of four.

Observing, Comparing, and Describing

1. Begin by having students share their knowledge of energy. The following questions are useful in guiding discussion:

What is energy? *(The ability to do work or to produce motion; a property of matter that can appear as motion, heat, light, chemical or nuclear energy, sound, magnetism, or electricity)*

Where is energy found? *(Wherever there is matter)*

How do we use energy in our daily lives? *(We get energy from food, we move, use heat, light, electrical energy, etc.)*

2. Tell students that energy can appear in many forms—as the energy of motion or in the form of heat and light. It can appear in the flow of electrical current or on an atomic or molecular scale as chemical energy. *Energy* is defined as "the ability to do work" or "the ability to make things move." Energy provides living things with the ability to grow and to reproduce. Light, heat, sound, magnetism, and electricity are all manifestations of energy.

3. Ask, "What forms of energy exist in this classroom? What specific examples of energy can you find?" Tell students to work in groups of four to list all of the examples of energy they can find in the room. Have each group select a member to record ideas on a sheet of writing paper.

4. Distribute writing paper, and have students begin. Circulate, and offer assistance as needed.

Drawing Conclusions

Have a member from each group share ideas. You may record these on the chalkboard. The following questions are useful in guiding discussion:

What examples of energy did your group find? *(Answers will vary.)*

What examples came most easily to mind? *(Probably the overhead electric lights, sunlight through the windows, heat from the ventilator, etc.)*

What examples were more difficult to identify? *(Probably air currents, chemical energy in our bodies which produces growth, heat energy from our bodies warming the air and the chairs, sounds from voices and classroom noises, etc.)*

Explaining the Phenomenon

When you run after a ball on a soccer field, you are full of energy. When you lie in bed, doing nothing at all, you are also full of energy. The slightest movement will transfer some of your energy to something else. When you raise your arm, your sheet moves and rustles. When you get out of bed, the place where you were lying is warm. When you speak, your vocal cords transfer the energy of their movement to the air. The air carries that energy to surrounding surfaces, from which it rebounds to your ears and to the ears of the person to whom you speak.

Every substance in the observable universe, whether it is living or nonliving, has energy. This energy can be manifested as motion, light, heat, sound, electrical or chemical energy, and so on. Every action in the universe happens because of a transfer of energy. You both hear and see because of the transfer of energy from one substance to another.

Creating

1. Tell students that one way artists express the quality of energy in drawing is through gesture drawing. Gesture drawing is a drawing made of quickly drawn lines that convey a sense of motion.

2. Explain the procedure:

A volunteer will stand on a table where he or she can be seen by everyone. The volunteer will strike an action pose, such as that of a baseball pitcher, dancer, weight lifter, and so on.

When the teacher says, "Begin," start drawing. First, quickly draw the overall shape or form of the figure.

Draw what you see, focusing primarily on outlines. Draw quickly, almost scribbling. Never allow your charcoal or felt-tip pen to stop. Try to record the shapes, lines, angles, and curves that you see without bothering with such details as facial features. Draw faster! Faster!

When 60 seconds is up and the teacher says, "Stop," put your charcoal or pen down.

A different volunteer will strike a new pose. Take a new sheet of paper. Draw another gesture drawing for 1 minute and then stop.

Repeat this procedure until you have used up 15 sheets of paper—15 drawings in 15 minutes.

3. When students understand the procedure, distribute a stack of 15 sheets of typing paper to each student. Select a volunteer to strike a pose, and have students begin. Circulate, and offer assistance as needed.

Evaluating

1. Ask students to look over their 15 gesture drawings and to select one that they feel most expresses energetic motion.

2. Display the gesture drawings for everyone to see. Ask students to notice and compare the different kinds of lines their classmates used to express energy. Have students find examples of drawings that express various levels of energy: high, medium, and low.

note

After the first few drawings, some students may protest, feeling that gesture drawing is a waste of time. Tell them to stop thinking and to keep on drawing. After a period of initial awkwardness, gesture drawings will soon become fun and interesting. With practice, they may even become powerful and expressive, like those of such artists as Rembrandt, Delacroix, and Degas.

Going Further

Have students generate a list of questions for further investigation. Examples of such questions are:

- *How can the technique of gesture drawing be applied to sculpture?* Students can create gesture figures from aluminum foil. Cut three lengths into a sheet of heavy-duty aluminum foil, 14" wide. Loosely crumple the two bottom sections to form legs, the top center section to form a head, the remaining top sections to form arms, and the middle to form the torso, as shown. Bend the hands and feet and position the figure into an action pose. Glue the feet to a sturdy index card to provide stability.

- *How can motion be measured?* Students can measure motion in terms of distance and time by using the formula:

$$\text{Speed} = \frac{\text{Distance}}{\text{Time}}$$

Students can calculate the speed of a snail, a pill bug, and an ant in centimeters per minute. They can measure out a length of 100 meters and calculate their own running speeds in meters per minute. Have students measure and compare the speeds of various organisms and objects. They can record their findings in a journal or logbook.

Additional Resources

Alexander, Kay. "Figures Posed for Action," in *Learning to Look and Create: The Spectra Program, Grade Four.* Palo Alto, Calif.: Dale Seymour, 1988.

Edwards, Betty. *Drawing on the Artist Within.* New York: Simon & Schuster, 1986.

Gravity

Overview

What is gravity, and how does it pull objects toward the earth? In this activity, students observe the acceleration of falling objects by dropping small quantities of paint onto paper from varying heights. By comparing their splatters with a set of mystery splatters, students are able to identify the height from which the mystery drops must have fallen. As artists, students then drop paint from varying heights to create abstract splatter paintings.

Student Objectives

- observe that the force of gravity pulls objects toward the earth and that objects increase in acceleration as they fall.

- experiment to discover how a set of mystery splatters was created.

- use tempera paint and the force of gravity to create splatter paintings on colored construction paper.

Materials

- thin, liquid tempera paint in assorted colors
- containers to hold the paint, such as cut-off milk cartons
- plastic straws, several per container of paint
- metersticks or meter tape, 1 per group of 4 students
- Logsheet 25: Mystery Splatters (page 186)
- cellophane tape, 6 lengths per group
- outdoor space where students can create their splatter paintings
- large sheet of butcher paper and masking tape
- newspapers to cover work areas
- colored construction paper, 12" x 18"
- ball

Getting Ready

1. Add sufficient water to the tempera paint to create a solution that will drop easily from a straw and splatter on paper. The thinned paint should have the consistency of ink.

2. If you do not have enough metersticks, have students use metric rulers to measure and cut strips of paper or yarn into meter lengths and mark off intervals of 2 cm.

3. Organize art materials and logsheets for easy distribution during the lesson.

4. Designate an area, either indoors or out, where students can create splatters. Although the paint will not fly upward onto students' clothing, small amounts of paint may splatter at ground level a distance of 60 cm or more from each student's paper. Have students tape large sheets of newspaper to the ground. Then have them tape their paper securely down in the center of the newspaper.

5. Place a large sheet of butcher paper on the floor of the classroom where students can see it easily. Place several containers of tempera paint and straws nearby.

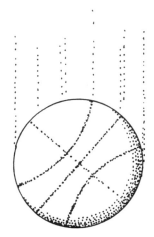

note
Students should be organized into groups of four.

Observing, Comparing, and Describing

1. Begin by having students share their knowledge of gravity. Have a student come to the front of the class and hold up a ball. Ask students to observe carefully as the volunteer bounces the ball several times. The following questions are useful in guiding discussion:

   What happens to the ball as it is released? *(It falls.)*

   Why does it fall down rather than up? *(Gravity)*

   What other kinds of objects fall when they are released? *(Stones, books, pencils, feathers; all objects fall to earth unless they are acted upon by a force that overcomes gravity.)*

2. Explain that a *force* is a push or a pull. *Gravity* is a force that pulls all objects toward the earth.

3. Show students a container of tempera paint. Place one end of a straw in the paint and cover the other end with your thumb. Remove the straw from the paint and hold it over the butcher paper. Tell students that when you lift your thumb from the end of the straw, a drop of paint will fall onto the paper.

4. Hold the straw 4 centimeters above the paper, and ask students to predict what the drop of paint will look like when it hits the paper.

5. Let the drop of paint fall. (It will make a fairly round spot on the paper.) Have students notice its size and appearance.

6. Ask students to predict what the paint will look like when it is dropped from 1 meter. Let the second drop fall next to the first. Have students compare its size and appearance to that of the first drop. (It will be larger and more splattered.)

7. Distribute copies of Logsheet 25: Mystery Splatters. Tell students that as they complete the logsheet, each person should share ideas and observations with others in the group.

8. Tell students that each group's task is to determine the height from which each of the mystery splatters was dropped. Each group will begin by investigating the appearance of drops from various heights.

9. Explain the procedure:

Let the first drop fall from very close to the paper, say 2 centimeters. Next to the splatter, record the height from which it fell.

Increase the height of the second drop by about 4 centimeters, so that you let the second drop fall from a height of 6 centimeters. Record the height next to the splatter.

Continue to increase the height of each drop by 4 centimeters (or a similarly small distance). Next to each splatter, record the height from which it fell. Continue until you have dropped paint from a height of 120 centimeters.

Compare the appearance of your drops with the mystery drops on the logsheet. From your group's results, determine the height from which each of the mystery splatters was dropped. Record your group's conclusions on the logsheet.

10. When students understand the procedure, take them to the designated area and have them begin. Circulate, and offer assistance as needed.

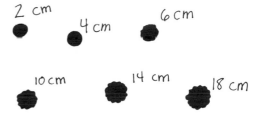

note

Students will notice that 120 centimeters is greater than the length of a meter. Have students brainstorm various ways to measure this height. (Measure the extra 20 cm on a strip of paper and add it to the meter; place the meterstick against a wall, mark the top with a finger, then move it 20 cm higher, etc.)

Drawing Conclusions

1. Gather students together. Have a member from each group share conclusions about the height of the mystery drops.

2. If there are large differences in opinion among the groups, help students speculate about what might have caused such differences (dropping technique, wind, thickness of the paint, etc.). Explain that differences that cause varying results in an experiment are called variables.

3. Have students speculate about why the size of the spatters increases with height. The following questions are useful in guiding discussion:

How does height affect the appearance of the splatters? *(The greater the fall, the larger and more spread out they appear.)*

Why do the splatters increase in size as the paint drops from a greater height? *(They hit the paper with greater force because the falling paint increases in speed as it falls toward the ground.)*

4. Tell students the heights from which the mystery splatters were dropped:

A—2 cm   B—58 cm   C—120 cm

D—90 cm   E—70 cm   F—14 cm

Explaining the Phenomenon

Most things fall to the ground when we let them go in midair. As they fall toward the earth, they increase in speed. The rate at which any object changes in speed as it is traveling in a given direction is called *acceleration*.

Galileo Galilei (1564–1642) conducted a series of experiments to discover how Earth's gravity affects things near the surface of our planet. He argued that if different objects fell without air or anything else to slow their motion, they would fall with the same acceleration. In other words, a rock and a leaf would reach the same speeds if they fell the same amount of time. Later experiments in which scientists dropped various objects in a vacuum confirmed Galileo's theory.

The value of acceleration toward the earth is given the symbol g and amounts to about 32 feet per second *per second*. In other words, the speed of a freely falling object increases by 32 feet per second for each second that it falls. At this rate, only 3 seconds of free fall would bring a skydiver to a speed of 66 miles per hour if there were no air resistance.

Creating

1. Tell students that artists make use of the force of gravity to create *splatter paintings*. A splatter painting is a painting made by dropping paint from varying heights onto paper, canvas, or some other surface.

2. Demonstrate the procedure:

Lay a sheet of construction paper in the center of a sheet of newspaper.

Use a straw to drop various colors of tempera paint onto the paper. Vary the height of the straw to release a combination of small, round drops and large, splattered ones.

Point out that the splattering of the paint creates a sense of energy and movement in the design.

Release larger quantities of paint as you move your arm in a circular motion. Tell students to drop the paint onto the paper in as many different ways as they can, being careful not to splatter paint farther than the edge of the newspaper.

Cover the area of the paper with splatters, leaving some of the colored background showing.

3. When students understand the procedure, take them to the designated area, distribute newspaper and art materials, and have them begin to paint. Circulate, and offer assistance as needed.

Evaluating

Display the dried paintings. Have students compare the size of the splatters created by their classmates and have them speculate about how they were made. Ask students to identify examples of designs in which the splattered paint creates a sense of energy.

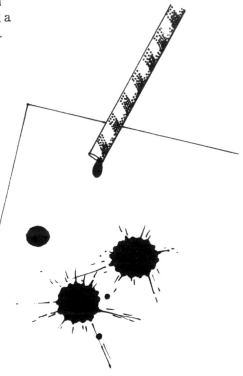

Going Further

Have students generate a list of questions for further investigation. Examples of such questions are:

- *How can the force of gravity be measured?* Help students understand that weight is the pull of earth's gravity on an object. Have students weigh a variety of objects and record the results in a journal or logbook.

- *What is free fall, or weightlessness?* Students can approximate free fall by strapping on a small backpack containing a book and hopping down from a chair. They will feel the pack's weight vanish from their shoulders as they are falling.

  For another demonstration, have each student fill a paper cup with water. As students hold the cups in their hands, they will feel its weight. Outdoors, have them use the straightened end of a paper clip to punch a small hole near the bottom. A stream of water will squirt straight out. Then, ask students to hold the cup by the rim and release it. The stream of water will vanish instantly as the cup and water fall freely toward the ground.

  News reporters often say astronauts are "weightless" when in orbit, but a more accurate description of their condition is to say they are in free fall. While in free fall, objects seem to have no weight *relative to each other.*

Additional Resources

Allison, Linda, and David Katz. "Splat Testing," in *Gee, Wiz!* Boston: Little, Brown, 1983.

Laithwaite, Eric. Force: *The Power Behind Movement.* New York: Watts, 1986.

Strongin, Herb. "Overcoming Gravity," in *Science on a Shoestring.* Menlo Park, Calif.: Addison-Wesley, 1991.

Wind

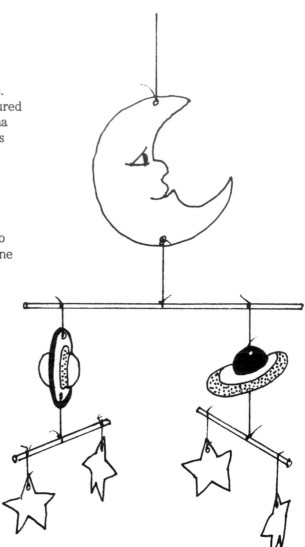

Overview

How does wind provide energy? In this investigation, students simulate the action of wind by blowing through drinking straws. They experiment to discover how much wind energy (as measured in puffs) is required to move such objects as a cotton ball, a lima bean, and a pebble a distance of one meter. As artists, students then create mobiles, sculptures that are set in motion by wind.

Student Objectives

- observe that wind energy can produce movement.

- experiment to discover how many puffs of air are required to move a cotton ball, a lima bean, and a pebble a distance of one meter.

- construct a balanced mobile sculpture.

Materials

- cotton balls, lima beans, and pebbles, 1 each per group of 4 students

- Logsheet 26: How Many Puffs? (page 187)

- pencils

- masking tape

- drinking straws

- metersticks or segments of yarn 1 m in length, 1 per group of 4 students

- tagboard, cut into 5" x 5" pieces, 7 pieces per student

- scissors

- thread, 1 spool per group of 4 students

- rods, 1 longer and two shorter, 3 per student, of such materials as dowels, bamboo sticks, or sections of wire coat hangers

- glue

- crayons

- scraps of colored construction paper, foil, or other such materials

- paper clips

- newspapers to cover work areas

Getting Ready

1. For each group of four students, organize the following set of materials: a cotton ball, a lima bean, a pebble, logsheets, pencils, four straws, a length of masking tape (about 6") and one meterstick (or a segment of yarn 1 m in length).

2. Cut tagboard into pieces approximately 5" x 5".

3. Obtain rods for the mobiles. Each student will need one long and two short rods. You can obtain dowels or lengths of bamboo from a local hardware or craft store. Or, have students bring in wire coat hangers and use a wire-cutter to cut each hanger into three lengths.

4. For each group of four students, organize a set of art materials: tagboard pieces, scissors, nylon thread or fishing line, rods (dowels, rigid wire lengths, etc.), glue, materials for decorating suspended forms (such as colored paper or foil), crayons, pencils, tape, and paper clips.

5. Cover work areas with newspaper.

6. Select an area of the classroom where students can hang finished mobiles.

note
Students should be organized into groups of four.

Observing, Comparing, and Describing

1. Begin by having students share their knowledge of wind energy. The following questions are useful in guiding discussion:

How is wind a source of energy? *(Its force can move such objects as sailing ships and windmills.)*

How do we use the force of wind in everyday life? *(To lift kites and paper airplanes; to provide extra push on a bicycle or skateboard; to dry clothes, etc.)*

What causes wind? *(As warm tropical air rises into the earth's atmosphere, cooler polar air moves in to replace it— that and the rotation of the earth results in wind.)*

2. Remind students that *energy* is the ability to do work or to make things move. *Wind* is a natural source of energy on earth.

3. Show students a cotton ball, a lima bean, and a pebble. Tell them that they will experiment to discover how much wind energy it takes to move each of the three objects a distance of one meter.

4. Ask students to predict which object will require the most energy to move. Record their predictions on the chalkboard with tally marks beside the words "Cotton," "Bean," and "Pebble."

Cotton   Bean   Pebble

               IIII I   IIII III

5. Distribute copies of Logsheet 26: How Many Puffs? Tell students that as they complete the logsheet, each person should share ideas and observations with others in the group.

6. Demonstrate the procedure:

Use a meterstick or a yarn segment to measure a distance of one meter on the floor. Mark each end of this distance with a short piece of masking tape.

Place a cotton ball on the "starting line."

Blow short puffs of air through a drinking straw to propel the cotton ball across the "finish line."

As you blow, count the number of puffs it takes for the cotton ball to travel the distance. Record the number on the logsheet.

Have each group member record the number of puffs required to move the cotton ball. Then calculate the group average and record the number on the logsheet.

Repeat the procedure for the lima bean and the pebble.

7. When students understand the procedure, distribute the materials, help each group select a suitable floor space, and have them begin. Circulate, and offer assistance as necessary.

Drawing Conclusions

Have a member from each group share the results. The following questions are useful in guiding discussion:

How does the shape of the object affect the number of puffs required to move it? (*An object presenting a greater amount of surface area to the wind source will have more air resistance and be easier to push.*)

How does the weight of the object affect the number of puffs required to move it? (*In the absence of air resistance or friction, a greater force is required to move an object of greater mass.*)

Did each team member move the same object with the same number of puffs? (*Probably not*) What factors might have caused differences? (*Such variables as puffing technique, position of the object, etc.*)

Creating

1. Tell students that a *mobile* is a suspended sculpture with parts that can be set in motion by air currents.

2. Draw a model of a mobile on the chalkboard, as shown. Point out that the model has three levels. There are four shapes suspended at the lowest level, two shapes suspended at the middle level, and a single shape suspended at the top.

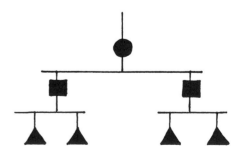

3. Demonstrate the procedure:

Use crayon to draw outlines of shapes on the tagboard pieces. Explain that students may fill in the outlines with crayon or by pasting pieces of colored paper, foil, or other material inside the outline.

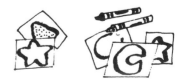

Cut out the outline drawings.

Carefully push a pencil point through each tagboard shape. Tie a length of thread to each. Make two holes in each of the top and middle level shapes, and attach two lengths of thread to each, as shown.

Attach the long rod to the thread hanging below the top shape. Tie the thread to the center of the rod and slide it back and forth to locate the center of balance. Secure it with a small piece of tape.

Suspend the two middle level shapes from either end of the long rod. Secure them in place with a piece of tape.

Suspend the small rods below the middle level shapes, and then suspend the lowest level shapes from either end of the small rods. Secure them in place with a piece of tape.

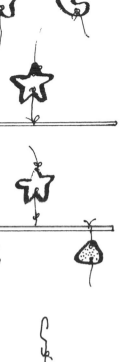

Have a partner hold the finished mobile. Adjust the threads as needed by removing the tape pieces and moving the threads until the mobile parts balance. When the mobile is balanced to satisfaction, remove the tape pieces and secure the threads with a spot of glue.

Pull open a paper clip so that it forms a hook. Attach this hook to the topmost thread of the mobile. Hang the finished mobile in a designated area of the classroom so that the glue can dry.

Evaluating

Ask students to observe and compare the mobiles created by their classmates. Questions to guide discussion are:

How was balance achieved in each mobile? *(Answers will vary.)*

What effect do the air currents in the classroom have on the mobiles? *(Answers will vary.)*

Going Further

Have students generate a list of questions for further investigation. Examples of such questions are:

- *How can we measure wind speed?* Students can build a simple *anemometer,* an instrument used to measure the speed of winds. Give students the following directions: First, cut diagonals into a large, sturdy piece of square paper. Turn the flaps inward, and insert a pin through the middle. Stick the pin through a small bead to act as a spacer, and push the pin into a stick. Color one arm of the windmill. As the windmill turns in the wind, count the number of times the colored arm goes around in 1 minute. The greater the number of rotations, the harder the wind is blowing.

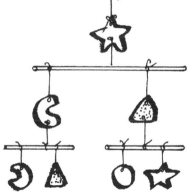

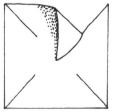

- *How can we detect air currents?* Students can detect small air currents in the classroom by blowing bubbles and noting the direction in which the bubbles move. Have students draw a map showing the location of school buildings, playground, field, outdoor structures, and so on. Using bubbles to discover the direction of the air currents either indoors or out, students can draw small arrows on their maps to record the direction in which the air is moving.

Additional Resources

Dorros, Arthur. *Feel the Wind.* New York: Crowell, 1988.

Kraul, Walter. *Earth, Water, Fire and Air.* Great Britain: Floris, 1984.

Lowery, Larry. "Meteorology," in *The Everyday Science Sourcebook.* Palo Alto, Calif.: Dale Seymour, 1985.

Reflection

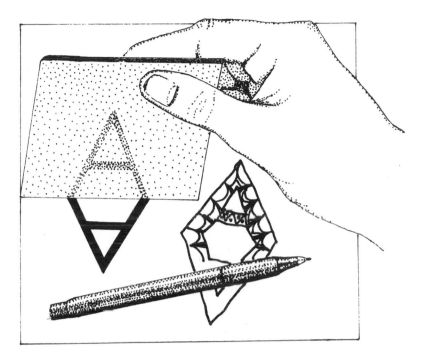

Overview

How is light reflected? Can we predict the angle of reflection? Students discover the answers to these questions by investigating the reflection of light with a mirror and flashlight. Using mirrors to alter the appearance of letters, they then create a secret code made up of patterned letters.

Student Objectives

- observe that light travels in straight lines; when light is reflected from a mirror, the angle of incidence equals the angle of reflection.

- use pen and ink to draw patterned letters.

Materials

- masking tape
- flashlight
- small square or rectangular mirrors
- scratch paper, several sheets per student
- white drawing paper, 9" x 12"
- colored pens or crayons
- pencils

Getting Ready

1. If small mirrors are not available at school, have students bring them from home. Square or rectangular mirrors are preferable.

2. Select an area of chalkboard that is easily visible to students. Tape a 5-foot piece of masking tape to the floor, running from the center of the chalkboard wall out toward the middle of the room.

3. Arrange materials for easy distribution during the lesson.

note
Students should be organized into groups of four.

Observing, Comparing, and Describing

1. Begin by having students share their knowledge of *light rays,* or beams of light. The following questions are useful in guiding discussion.

What can produce a ray of light? *(Flashlight, movie projector, lighthouse, sunlight penetrating rain clouds, spotlight, etc.)*

How would you describe the appearance of a ray of light? *(As a narrow beam of light traveling in a straight line)*

What kinds of conditions make light rays most visible? *(Darkness; small particles in the air to catch the light, such as water vapor, smoke, dust, etc.)*

2. Perform this demonstration:

Have a volunteer come to the front of the room and stand at the end of the masking tape, facing the chalkboard. Give the student a mirror, and have him or her hold it so that it faces the chalkboard.

Have another volunteer stand at the other end of the tape with his or her back to the wall. Give this volunteer a flashlight.

Darken the room somewhat, and challenge the two volunteers to hold the mirror and flashlight so that the light from the flashlight strikes the mirror and reflects directly back onto itself.

3. Have the class notice how the light ray is being reflected. The following questions are useful in guiding discussion:

What do you notice about the way they are holding the flashlight and mirror? *(Directly facing each other)*

What must they do to reflect the light right back onto the flashlight? *(Aim the ray of light into the center of the mirror; hold the mirror directly in front of the flashlight and perfectly parallel to the chalkboard.)*

What would happen if the mirror were tilted? *(The light ray would be reflected elsewhere.)*

4. Have the volunteer holding the mirror remain in position, and ask the other volunteer to turn off the flashlight and step 1 ft to the right. Ask, "When the light shines into the mirror now, where will the reflected ray land on the wall?"

5. Distribute a length of masking tape to each group of four students. Ask each group to make a prediction by marking the spot on the wall with a small piece of tape. When the flashlight is on, have students discuss the result.

6. Have the student with the flashlight step 1 ft farther to the right. Again, have each group make a prediction by marking a spot on the wall with tape. Repeat this procedure several times.

Drawing Conclusions

Ask students to share their group's strategy for making accurate predictions about where the reflected ray will fall.

Explaining the Phenomenon

Light that is reflected travels in a straight line. The ray that strikes the mirror is called the *incident ray,* and the angle it makes with the mirror is called the *angle of incidence.* The ray that is reflected from the mirror is called the *reflected ray,* and the angle it makes with the mirror is called the *angle of reflection.* The angle of incidence always equals the angle of reflection.

note

For more information about the reflection of light, see "Light: Background Information" on page 152.

Creating

1. Distribute drawing paper and mirrors (or have students get the mirrors they brought from home). Tell students that because reflected light travels in straight lines, tilting a mirror can make things look very different. Have students write a letter in pencil, as shown.

2. Have students move the mirror around and notice how they can alter the appearance of the letter. Depending on how they move the mirror, the letter might look like any of the letters shown.

3. Tell students that they can use their mirrors to create a secret code. Demonstrate the procedure:

Decide on a secret message to encode. Draw the letter of the first word on a sheet of scratch paper.

Hold a mirror next to the letter, and tilt the mirror until you have altered the letter's appearance.

With pencil, draw the shape you see in the mirror on a sheet of drawing paper.

Tell students to repeat the procedure until the entire secret message has been recorded on the drawing paper.

4. Demonstrate how to use colored pens or crayons to go back over the letters and embellish them with patterns. Define a *pattern* as "a regular arrangement of repeated shapes, lines, or colors." Ask students for suggestions about various patterns they might draw.

5. When students understand the procedure, distribute the materials and have them begin. Encourage them to practice making altered letters before they begin work on their secret code.

6. Circulate, and offer assistance as needed.

Evaluating

Have students notice and discuss the patterns used by their classmates. Discuss similarities and differences and the use of repetition in the patterns.

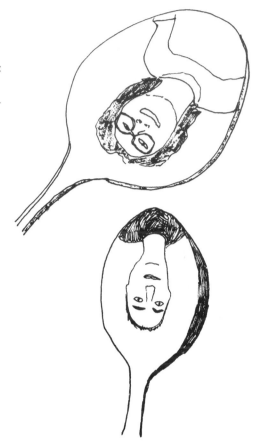

Going Further

Have students generate a list of questions for further investigation. Examples of such questions are:

- *What effects can be created using two mirrors?* Have students explore the effects of two mirrors. Give them the following directions: Stand two mirrors on edge so that they are parallel to each other. Keep them upright by wedging them in some modeling clay on a table. The mirrors should be facing each other. Place a coin between the mirrors and look over one mirror into the other. (Students will see many coins.) Use cellophane tape to hinge two mirrors together, and set them up so that they are at right angles to each other. Place a coin between the mirrors, and note the number of images formed. Make smaller and smaller angles, and observe what happens to the number of images.

- *How do curved surfaces reflect light?* Students can observe and compare their reflections in such objects as metal coffeepots, spoons, and metal bowls. Have them draw a self-portrait as reflected from the concave (inward-curving) side of a spoon. Then have them draw a self-portrait as reflected from the convex (outward curving) side.

Additional Resources

Allison, Linda, and David Katz. *Gee, Wiz!* Boston: Little, Brown, 1983.

Simon, Seymour. *Mirror Magic.* New York: Lothrop, 1980.

White, Lawrence, & Ray Broekel. *Optical Illusions.* New York: Watts, 1986.

Refraction

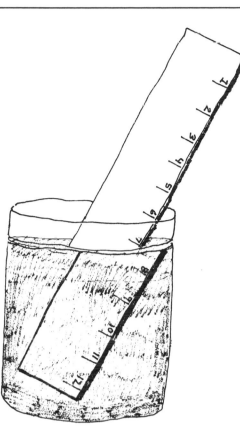

Overview

How does the refraction of light alter the appearance of objects?
From a certain angle, a pencil that is half- submerged in water
looks as if it has been sliced in half. Change the angle, and it
assumes a perpendicular shape, like the letter L. In this activity,
students use the technique of drawing through observation to
explore the effects of refraction.

Student Objectives

- observe that refraction occurs when the path of light is bent as
  it moves from one medium to another, as from air to water or
  glass.

- use drawing techniques of looking, studying, and eye-hand
  coordination.

Materials

- water

- transparent plastic cups

- long, narrow objects, such as watercolor brushes, rulers, or craft
  sticks

- pencils

- Logsheet 27: Refraction (page 188)

Getting Ready

1. Pour water into each transparent plastic cup until half full.

2. Arrange cups, logsheets, and such objects as rulers, brushes, or
craft sticks for easy distribution during the lesson.

note
Students work individually in this
lesson.

Observing and Comparing

1. Begin by having students share their knowledge of light energy.
The following questions are useful in guiding discussion:

What is light? *(Radiant energy)*

What are the sources of light? *(Sun, stars, fire,
phosphorescence, bioluminescence, etc.)*

How does light travel? *(In straight lines; in waves)*

How is light reflected? *(It strikes a smooth surface and
rebounds.)*

What kinds of substances can light travel through? *(Any
transparent or translucent substances, including a
vacuum, air, water, crystal, glass, etc.)*

2. Tell students that when light passes from water to air or vice versa, it bends. This bending of light can alter the appearance of objects.

3. Distribute the cups of water. Have students stand a pencil in the water. Ask them to look at the pencil from the side and to describe what they see.

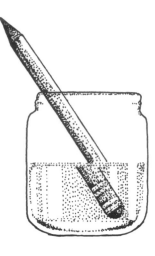

Creating

1. Explain that one way to observe something thoroughly is to draw it. Distribute Logsheet 27: Refraction. Tell students that they will draw four different illustrations of the pencil standing in the cup.

2. Help students understand that to make something look real, one must look at it very carefully. This involves three steps: looking, studying, and drawing.

3. Explain the steps of looking, studying, and drawing:

Looking at an object is the first step in observation. In looking, the artist notices the whole form of the object in its environment—its overall appearance.

Studying an object is the second step. In studying, the artist notices the various parts and details of the object. He or she carefully observes the object's line, shape, color, texture, and size.

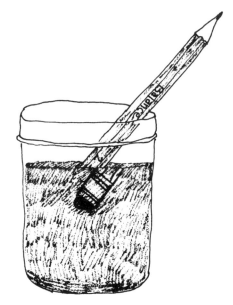

Drawing is the third step. In drawing, the artist first captures the whole form of the object, and then adds details. The artist draws for several seconds, looks and studies, and then draws again. This process is repeated over and over again until details have been added and the drawing is completed.

4. When students understand the procedure, have them begin to draw. Circulate, and offer assistance as needed. To help students stay on task, you may begin the drawing activity by saying aloud, "Look, look, look, look," for four beats, and then say, "Draw, draw, draw, draw, draw, draw," for six beats.

5. After students have completed the first drawing, ask them to move or hold the cup so that the pencil looks completely different. Model this by holding up a cup, looking at it from various angles, and making such comments as, "Now it looks large on the bottom," or "Now it looks like two pencils."

6. Have students select an angle from which to do a second drawing on the logsheet. Repeat the steps of looking, drawing, and studying.

7. Ask students if they can find still different angles from which to make a third and fourth drawing (looking at the cup from above or below, for example). Follow the steps of looking, drawing, and studying for the remaining two drawings.

Drawing Conclusions

Ask students to share their observations with the class. The following questions are useful in guiding discussion.

Was there an angle from which the pencil looked normal?
(From directly above or below the cup)

At what angle did it look bent? Broken? Like two pencils?
(Answers will vary.)

Explaining the Phenomenon

Rays of light change their direction when they pass at an angle
from one transparent substance into another, such as from air to
water. This bending of light is called *refraction.* Refraction occurs
because light moves more slowly through some substances than
through others.

note

For more information on refraction,
see "Light: Background Information"
on page 152.

Going Further

Have students generate a list of questions for further investigation.
Examples of such questions are:

■ *In what other ways can refraction fool our eyes?* You can
demonstrate a "magic trick" that works because of refraction:
First, place a coin in a paper cup so that the edge of the coin
just touches the edge of the cup. Have a student step close
enough to the cup to see the coin clearly. Second, have the
student step back to the point where the coin completely
disappears. While the student is holding this position, have
another student pour water into the cup slowly and carefully so
that it won't move the coin.

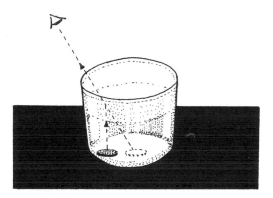

The first student will see the coin emerge into view. When the
water was added, light reflected from the coin was bent as it
passed from the water into the air. The coin now seems to be in
a different position from where it actually is.

■ *How can we observe refraction outdoors?* Have students
watch the sun set in the evening. Have them record a
description of its shape and color from the time its rim first
touches the horizon to the time it disappears. The next day
have students share their observations with the class. Explain
that refraction exists in our atmosphere. Rays from the sun
entering nearly horizontally are bent most. This happens each
time the sun rises or sets. At sunset you can sometimes watch
the sun flatten a bit and finally touch the horizon. It flattens
because the rays from the bottom of the sun pass through a bit
more of the thickest part of the atmosphere, so they bend more
toward the zenith than do the rays from the top of the sun. In
fact, when the sun is at such a low angle, *all* of its rays are bent.
As a result, the sun itself is just *below* the horizon when you are
seeing its image just *touch* the horizon. The sun seems to
change to orange or red because of selective reflection.

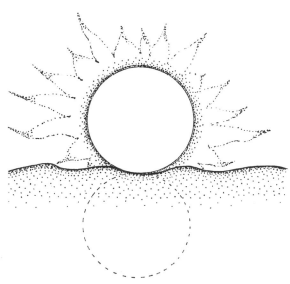

Additional Resources

Alexander, Kay. "Drawing the Line," in *Learning to Look and Create: The Spectra Program, Grade Four.* Palo Alto, Calif.: Dale Seymour, 1989.

"Magnifying Experience," in *Scienceworks.* The Ontario Science Centre. Menlo Park, Calif.: Addison-Wesley, 1986.

Afterimages and Animation

Overview

How does the retina of the eye react to light? In this investigation, students experiment to discover the effects of persistent vision, the holding action of the retina. By observing a variety of colors and comparing the afterimages that result, students discover how the action of light-sensitive cells in the retina determines the way we see color. As artists, students then apply the principle of persistent vision in creating minimovies from flip books.

Student Objectives

- observe and compare the effects of persistent vision.

- create minimovies from flip books to show animation.

Materials

- Logsheet 28: Persistent Vision (page 189)

- flashlights, 1 per student or student pair

- crayons: black, blue, red, green, yellow, orange—1 set per group of 4 students

- drawing paper, cut into 4 1/2" x 6" sheets, 3 or 4 per student

- white paper, unlined, from which to prepare a 20–30 page flip book, about 1 1/2" x 2 1/2"—1 per student

- stapler

- pencils or black fine-tip felt pens

note

If flashlights are not available, the investigation may be conducted outdoors on a sunny day.

Getting Ready

1. Gather as many flashlights as you can. You might ask students to bring these from home, and you can provide extras to those who need them.

2. Organize flashlights, crayons, and drawing paper for easy distribution during the "Observing, Comparing, and Describing" portion of the lesson.

3. For each student, prepare a 20–30 page flip book, about 1 1/2" x 2 1/2". You can have several students make these in advance by stapling together pieces of plain white paper.

4. Organize flip books and pencils or fine felt-tip pens for easy distribution during the "Creating" portion of the lesson.

note

Students should be organized into groups of four.

Observing, Comparing, and Describing

1. Begin by having students share their knowledge of *afterimages*, images of objects that remain after we have closed our eyes. The following questions are useful in guiding discussion.

What kinds of things can you see with your eyes closed? *(Spots, colors, afterimages of bright lights, etc.)*

What do you see after someone takes your picture with a flash camera? *(Spots, colors)*

What do you see when the lights suddenly go off in your house? *(May see afterimages of lights)*

2. Tell students that they will work in groups of four to investigate some of the effects of *persistent vision*. Explain that persistent vision causes us to see afterimages, pictures that register in the brain for a fraction of a second after we have ceased looking at them.

3. Distribute copies of Logsheet 28: Persistent Vision. Tell students that as they complete the logsheet, each person should share ideas and observations with others in the group.

4. Demonstrate the procedure:

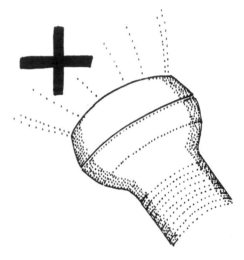

Use a black crayon to draw a thick black cross in the middle of a sheet of paper.

Shine a flashlight on the black cross. Stare at the cross for 30 seconds without blinking. Keep your eyes steady.

When 30 seconds have passed, close your eyes and shine the light from the flashlight on your face for approximately 10 seconds. What do you see? Use crayons to draw a picture on the logsheet of the colored afterimage you observe.

Repeat the experiment using different colored crayons: red, yellow, blue, green, and orange. Does everyone in your group see the same colors?

5. When students understand the procedure, distribute paper, crayons, and flashlights, and have them begin the investigation. Circulate, and offer assistance as needed.

Drawing Conclusions

Have students share their observations. The following questions are useful in guiding discussion:

What did you observe when experimenting with the black cross? *(The image is visible with eyes closed.)*

What differences did you observe when experimenting with different colored crayons? *(A black cross produces a white afterimage; a red cross produces a green afterimage; a yellow cross produces a purple afterimage; a blue cross an orange afterimage, a green cross a red afterimage, and an orange cross a blue afterimage.)*

Did everyone in each group see the same colors? *(Not necessarily—the same color can be identified as green by one individual or turquoise by another; some individuals may be colorblind.)*

Explaining the Phenomenon

You see by means of a coating of light-sensitive cells inside the back of the eye. This coating is called the *retina*. When light energy hits these cells, they become excited and send a message to the brain.

Because it takes some time to do this and for the cells to calm down again, the picture they receive does not vanish instantly. It lasts for a fraction of a second. This holding action of the retina is called *persistent vision*.

When you stare at a red object for a period of time and then close your eyes, the afterimage that appears will be green. This happens because the color receptors in your retina that are most responsive to red have been excited for some time. It is as if they have become tired. When your eyelid covers your eye, the tired receptors in your retina can no longer react to the red portion of light from the object. What you see is the afterimage with red subtracted from it, which your brain interprets as green.

The phenomenon of persistent vision enables you to see a series of pictures as a moving picture, or movie. As you watch a movie filmed with a home movie camera, you are seeing about 18 separate picture frames per second, in sequence. Your eye sees a single frame as it is projected at this speed, but the image remains in your mind as the next frame is registered, giving you an impression of continuous motion.

Creating

1. Explain that an artist who draws illustrations for a movie is called an *animator*. Tell students that they will be working as animators to create a small movie from a flip book.

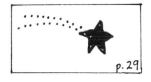

2. Demonstrate the procedure:

Draw a simple figure or object on the last page of a small flip book.

On each preceding page, trace the figure while adding a small change to indicate action, such as an arm moving up and down, a leg lifting, and so on.

Flip the pages, and the figure will appear to move. Point out that the more drawings there are in a sequence and the smaller the changes are from drawing to drawing, the smoother the action will appear.

3. When students understand the procedure, distribute the flip books and pencils or fine-tip felt pens, and have them begin. Circulate, and offer assistance as needed. Remind students to begin on the *last* page of their flip book.

Evaluating

Have students trade flip books and observe the sequence of action created by their classmates. Ask students to identify examples of smooth action sequences.

Going Further

Have students generate a list of questions for further investigation. Examples of such questions are:

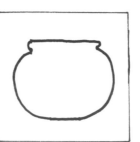

- *How else can the effects of persistent vision be observed?* Students can create a device called a thaumatrope, one of the early inventions that led to movies. Give students the following directions: First, cut out a 2-inch square of paper. Draw a fish on one side and a large fish bowl on the other. Stick the paper square to the side of a pencil eraser with a push pin. Hold the pencil up between your hands. Roll it back and forth so that both sides of the paper flip into view. When the paper flips fast enough, the fish will appear to be inside the bowl.

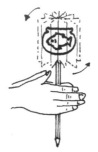

- *How else can the effects of persistent vision alter the way we see colors?* Students can investigate further the phenomenon of colored afterimages. With crayons, draw a United States flag with the following colors: black for the stars, orange for the background, and alternately black and green for the stripes. Have students stare at this flag for approximately 30 seconds and then move their eyes to a sheet of white paper. The afterimage of the flag will appear red, white, and blue.

Additional Resources

Alexander, Kay. "Walt Disney and the Art of Animation," in *Learning to Look and Create: The Spectra Program, Grade Five.* Palo Alto, Calif.: Dale Seymour, 1988.

Allison, Linda, and David Katz. "Movies on the Brain," in *Gee, Wiz!* Boston: Little, Brown, 1983.

DiSpezio, Michael. *Science Video Adventures, Module 1: Optical Illusions.* Menlo Park, Calif.: Addison-Wesley, 1993.

Stein, Sara. "Sights," in *The Science Book.* New York: Workman, 1979.

• •

Light: Background Information

Light is a form of radiant energy. When the colors of light are separated, they produce a rainbow spread of colors called the *spectrum.* Some light rays are invisible to the human eye. *Infrared rays* have wavelengths longer than the waves of the visible spectrum, and *ultraviolet rays* have shorter wavelengths than visible radiation. White light is the combination of the colors of light all traveling together.

When sunlight strikes your favorite blue shirt, all of the colors of the rainbow shine on the material, yet the blue wavelengths are the ones you see when you look at it. The other wavelengths of light are absorbed by the material. This reradiation of only certain wavelengths is called *selective reflection.* Selective reflection plays a part in the light we see from the atmosphere. Particles from volcanic emissions, forest fires, and air pollution often reflect light that colors local skies.

You can see the sharp beam of a spotlight in a theater because smoke, dust, and the air itself scatter a small portion of the light from the beam as it travels. Without material to reflect it, light is invisible to our eyes. Light rays travel in a straight line. Experiments have shown that the speed of light in a vacuum is about 186,282.03 miles per second (or about 299,792.46 kilometers per second). At this speed, light appears to us to move instantaneously.

This page reflects more than half of the visible light falling on it. But the surface of the paper is uneven, and so it *diffuses* the light—that is, the light reflected from it is scattered in many directions. In contrast, the surface of a mirror reflects light fairly uniformly. Light rays hitting the mirror's surface perpendicularly reflect straight back along their incoming paths. Any rays that strike a mirror at an angle to a perpendicular line drawn from the mirror's surface will reflect at an equal angle. The *angle of incidence* made by the path of the incoming ray is equal to the *angle of reflection* made by the outgoing ray. In other words, light rays are reflected from a mirror as a pool ball might rebound from the side of a billiard table.

When you dip one end of a straw into water at an angle to the surface, the image you see of the submerged part appears bent because its image is displaced. This occurs because the light coming from the submerged portion of the straw changes direction as it leaves the water, in a process called *refraction*. Refraction occurs because light takes more time to travel through water than through air. In air at sea level, light travels at about 99.97% of its speed in a vacuum; in water it is about 75% as fast, and in glass or quartz, 65%, and in a diamond, 42%. Light refracts, or changes directions, when it angles out of one material into another where it travels with a different speed.

A *mirage* is an image of light that has been misplaced by refraction. A hot surface, such as a road or sand dune, warms the air that touches it, forming a thin blanket of hot air next to the surface. Light entering this hotter air travels faster than it travels through the cooler air above it because there are fewer molecules to slow the light. When light angles into this hot layer, it increases speed and bends away from the surface. The mirage comes from the light from the sky or from any objects just above the road from your line of sight.

Designing a Desert House

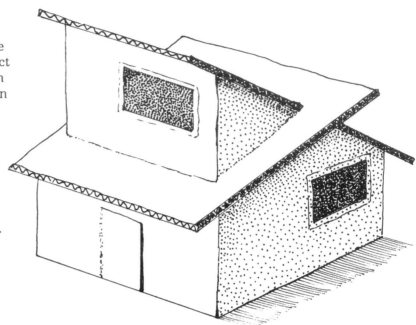

Overview

How can we design a house to stay cool in the desert? In this investigation, students conduct two controlled experiments to discover which materials provide the most effective insulation against solar energy. They then apply their knowledge by designing a small model house that will stay cool in sunlight.

Student Objectives

- conduct two controlled experiments to compare the effect of such variables as exterior color and insulation on the indoor temperature of a model house.

- design and construct a model house.

Materials

- milk cartons, quart-sized, 1 per student
- Logsheet 29: Heat Experiments (page 190)
- construction paper, 18" x 24", 2 sheets of white and 1 each of black, blue, and yellow per group of 4 students
- scissors
- pencils
- white glue
- alcohol thermometers, 4 per group of 4 students
- tape, 1 roll per group of 4 students
- cloth, at least 18" x 24", 1 length per group of 4 students
- cotton balls, 1 bag per group of 4 students
- polystyrene trays, several per student
- cardboard, several pieces per student
- newspapers to cover work areas
- rulers
- tagboard, 1 large piece per student
- clear plastic wrap, a 1-ft length per student
- straight pins, at least 1 dozen per student
- tempera paint, various colors
- containers to hold paint, such as cut-off milk cartons

- brushes
- scratch paper

Getting Ready

1. Collect quart-sized milk cartons so that you have one for each student. Students can bring these from home (cleaned). Also collect lengths of cloth—you will need a piece at least 18" x 24" for each group of four students.

2. Obtain polystyrene trays from your local butcher and box cardboard from your local grocery. You will need four or five polystyrene trays and one cardboard box for each group of four students. Enlist students' help in bringing these items from home.

3. For each group of four students, gather the following materials: four milk cartons, logsheets, two pieces of white construction paper and one each of black, blue, and yellow, scissors, pencils, glue, four thermometers, tape, and cloth, cotton balls, polystyrene, and cardboard. Organize these materials for easy distribution during the "Observing, Comparing, and Describing" portion of the lesson.

4. Cover work areas with newspapers.

5. Select an area, either indoors or out, where students can place their experimental houses. The houses must be placed where sunlight falls on them.

6. Organize the following materials for easy distribution during the "Creating" portion of the lesson: rulers, polystyrene trays, cardboard, tagboard, clear plastic wrap, scissors, white glue, straight pins, various insulating materials, tempera paint, and brushes.

Observing, Comparing, and Describing

1. Begin by having students share their knowledge of heat energy. The following questions are useful in guiding discussion:

What are the sources of heat energy? *(Light, friction, electricity, chemical reactions, the earth's interior, etc.)*

How does heat energy travel from one place to another? *(It passes between molecules because of their contact; it radiates.)*

How do we keep cool outdoors in hot weather? *(Wear less clothing; wear white or other light colors, etc.)*

What materials in this building help keep it cool in hot weather? *(Such materials as insulation in the walls, light-colored exterior paint, etc.)*

2. Tell students that they will conduct two experiments to discover what kinds of materials help keep a house cool in hot weather.

note

This investigation easily can be divided into three or four sessions. Students can spend two sessions conducting the experiments and one session (or more) designing and constructing the model houses.

note

Students should be organized into groups of four.

Explain that before an architect builds a house, he or she first experiments with small models.

3. Ask students to describe some of the ways houses can differ (shape, size, color, number of windows, etc.). Tell students that the first experiment will focus on one variable—the color of the house.

4. Distribute copies of Logsheet 29: Heat Experiments. Tell students that as they complete the logsheet, each person should share ideas and observations with others in the group.

5. Demonstrate the procedure:

Wrap a piece of colored construction paper around a milk carton to determine its perimeter. Trim the paper to exactly cover the perimeter of the carton.

Glue the paper to the carton. Cover three more cartons, each with a different color. Every group of four students should have a black, blue, yellow, and white carton house.

Place a thermometer inside each carton house. Record each carton's starting temperature on the logsheet.

Seal the cartons tightly closed with tape. Do not allow any openings where air can get in.

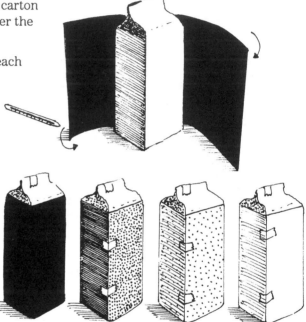

6. When students understand the procedure, distribute the materials and have them begin. Circulate, and offer assistance as needed.

7. After each group has finished preparing the cartons and has recorded the starting temperatures, direct students to place their carton houses in a designated sunny area, either indoors or out, for 10 minutes.

8. At the end of the 10-minute period, tell students to open the cartons, read the thermometers, and record the final temperatures on the logsheets. Show students how to calculate the net temperature change for each carton as follows:

Final temperature   _____

minus   −

Starting temperature   _____

equals   _____

9. Have students write their conclusions on the logsheet.

Drawing Conclusions

Have a member from each group share the group's results. (Cartons wrapped in black produce the greatest temperature rise, followed by blue and then yellow. White produces the smallest rise in temperature.)

Observing, Comparing, and Describing

1. Tell students that the second experiment will focus on another variable—insulation. Explain that an *insulating material* is a material through which heat travels slowly. An effective insulating material will prevent the heat outside the carton from reaching the interior.

2. Demonstrate the procedure:

Remove the construction paper from each carton.

Glue a different material to the outside of each carton: cover one with cloth, one with cotton balls that have been slightly stretched out and flattened, one with polystyrene, and one with cardboard.

Cover the insulated cartons with white construction paper so that each is the same color.

Place a thermometer inside each carton house. Record the starting temperature of each carton on the logsheet.

Seal the cartons tightly closed with tape. Do not allow any openings where air can get in.

3. When students understand the procedure, distribute the materials and have them begin. Circulate, and offer assistance as needed.

4. After each group has finished preparing the cartons and has recorded the temperatures, direct students to place their carton houses in the designated sunny area for another 10 minutes.

5. At the end of the 10-minute period, tell students to open the cartons, read the thermometers, record the final temperatures, and calculate the net temperature changes on the logsheets.

6. Have students write their conclusions on the logsheets.

Drawing Conclusions

Have a member from each group share the group's results. *(Polystyrene and cotton are more effective insulators than are cardboard or cloth.)*

Explaining the Phenomenon

Sunlight carries energy that warms the ground, the oceans, and the air. On a sunny day, a black jacket feels warmer to the touch than a white one. This is because the color black absorbs virtually all of the light energy that strikes it. You feel this light energy as heat. On the other hand, a white material reflects virtually all of the light that strikes it. The darker the color, the more light energy it absorbs. The lighter the color, the more light energy it reflects.

Buildings can be kept cool or warm through the use of insulating materials. Different materials conduct heat at different rates. Your bare feet will feel colder on a tile floor than on a wooden one at the same temperature because tile *conducts,* or carries heat faster. Your feet feel cold because the tile is carrying heat quickly away from them. An *insulating material* is a poor conductor of heat; in other words, it conducts heat very slowly. Polystyrene is a good example of an insulating material, which is why it has been so often used in the manufacture of disposable coffee cups.

note

For more information, see "Light: Background Information" on page 152 and "The Thermometer: Background Information" on page 160.

Creating

1. Tell students that they each will design and construct a small model house for a desert environment. They should design the house so that its walls and windows are shielded from the hot rays of the sun. They should use insulating materials and light colors to help keep it cool.

2. Explain that they must follow several rules in designing their houses:

   The base of the house must fit within a 9" x 12" rectangle.

   Three sides of the house must have at least one window each.

   The house must have at least one door that can open and shut.

   The house may have two stories but may be no taller than 10 inches.

3. Explain the procedure:

   First, sketch some building ideas on scratch paper. Try to create contrasts in size and shape to avoid a simple boxlike form.

   Decide on a shape for the base, or floor, of the house. Check to be sure the base fits within a 9" x 12" rectangle. Cut the base out of cardboard, tagboard, polystyrene, or other sturdy material.

   Decide on the structure of the exterior walls and the placement of windows and doors. Cut out the wall shapes. Cut windows into the walls. Cover the windows with clear pieces of plastic wrap. Glue or tape the plastic to the inside surface of the wall.

   Add the exterior walls to the base by gluing the pieces, and then holding them together with straight pins until the glue dries.

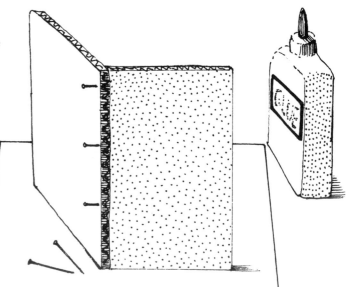

You may add insulating material to the inside surfaces of the exterior walls.

Add interior walls to create rooms. Glue the pieces, and then hold them together with straight pins until the glue dries. Add a second floor to create a second story if you wish. (Be sure the finished house stands no taller than 10 inches.) You may add insulating material to the surfaces of interior walls.

Add the roof. You may add insulating material to the underside of the roof. You may cover the roof with paint or other material.

Paint the house.

4. When students understand the procedure, distribute the materials and have them begin. Circulate, and offer assistance as needed.

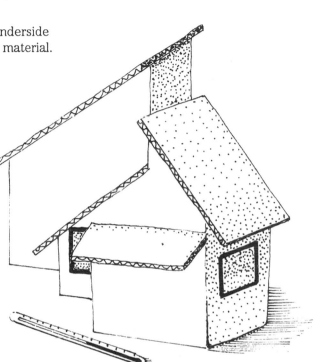

Evaluating

1. Display the finished models for everyone to see. Have students compare the various designs used by their classmates.

2. In the classroom, have each student position a thermometer in the center of his or her house and record the temperature. Then place the houses outdoors in sunlight. Near the houses, place an uncovered thermometer to serve as a control sample. After 10 minutes, have students read the thermometers to discover the indoor temperatures of their houses. How much did the temperature rise? Compare this with the temperature of the control thermometer. Were the houses effective in keeping relatively cool? Which designs and materials were the most effective?

Going Further

Have students generate a list of questions for further investigation. Examples of such questions are:

■ *How can windows be used to heat buildings with solar energy?* Have students cut a window, about 1" x 2", into one side of a quart milk carton. Cover the window with clear plastic. Lay the carton on its side in the sunlight, and place a thermometer on the floor of the carton so that it can be read easily. Have students record the temperatures reached when the window faces toward or away from the sun. Have students vary the size of the window and alter the position of the carton outdoors so that they can find the most effective way to heat the carton.

■ *How can solar energy be used to heat water?* Students can create a simple solar water heater by placing a quantity of water in an aluminum pie pan and setting the pan in sunlight. They then can experiment to discover whether an uncovered aluminum pan or a pan covered with clear plastic wrap produces the warmer water. They will observe the results of the greenhouse effect as the temperature of the covered water rises higher than that of the uncovered water.

Additional Resources

Alexander, Kay. "Form Follows Function," in *Learning to Look and Create: The Spectra Program, Grade Four.* Palo Alto, Calif.: Dale Seymour, 1988.

Gould, Alan. *Hot Water and Warm Homes from Sunlight.* University of California, Berkeley, Calif.: Lawrence Hall of Science, 1986.

Rahn, Joan Elma. *Keeping Warm, Keeping Cool.* New York: Atheneum, 1983.

• •

The Thermometer: Background Information

In 1592, Galileo constructed the first temperature-measuring device— the thermoscope. It was more than 125 years later before the German scientist Daniel Gabriel Fahrenheit invented the first accurate one.

Early instrument makers could not agree on whether water, mercury, or alcohol worked best. Individual thermometers varied enormously in their recording of the same temperature in the same place. To further complicate matters, everyone seemed to use a different degree scale. By the 18th century, about 20 different scales were in use.

The two most familiar scales used today are Fahrenheit and Celsius, both of which take the boiling and freezing points of water as their standards of reference. The Celsius scale was invented by Anders Celsius of Sweden in 1742. It takes zero as the freezing point of water and 100 degrees as the boiling point.

Logsheet Blackline Masters

Logsheet 1

Investigating Solids

1. Test each solid for *hardness*. Rank each solid from very soft to very hard.

2. Test each solid for *flexibility*. Rank each solid from very flexible to very rigid.

3. Test each solid for *adhesiveness*. Rank each solid from very adhesive to nonadhesive.

Very soft	**Very flexible**	**Very adhesive**
1. _____	1. _____	1. _____
2. _____	2. _____	2. _____
3. _____	3. _____	3. _____
4. _____	4. _____	4. _____
5. _____	5. _____	5. _____
6. _____	6. _____	6. _____
7. _____	7. _____	7. _____
8. _____	8. _____	8. _____
9. _____	9. _____	9. _____
10. _____	10. _____	10. _____
Very hard	**Very rigid**	**Nonadhesive**

 LESSON 2

Logsheet 2

Comparing Liquids

1. Describe each liquid's appearance, odor, and texture. _____

Catsup

_____

Syrup

_____

Water

_____

Milk

_____

2. Order the liquids by *weight* and *viscosity,* or thickness.
Rank the liquids below.

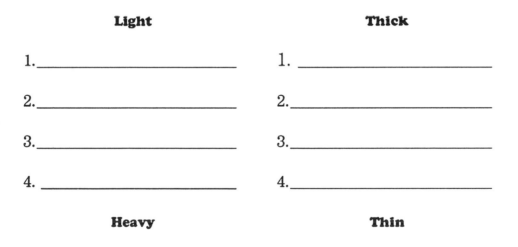

Light		**Thick**	
1._____		1._____	
2._____		2._____	
3._____		3._____	
4._____		4._____	
Heavy		**Thin**	

Logsheet 3

Comparing Loam and Clay

Answer the questions below.	Make quick sketches below— larger than life-size. Draw the things you find in the loam
What things can you find in the loam? What is the loam's appearance, odor, and texture?	
What things can you find in the clay? What is the clay's appearance, odor, and texture?	

LESSON 5

Logsheet 4

Backyard Creatures

Write a description of each animal below.	Make a quick sketch of each animal below—larger than life-size.
Animal 1	
Animal 2	
Animal 3	

Logsheet 5

Fish Anatomy

Write a description of each part below.	Make quick sketches below.
Dorsal fins	
Caudal fin	
Pectoral fin	
Gill	
Lateral line	

 LESSON 7

Logsheet 6

Dissecting a Chicken Leg

Answer the questions below.	Make quick sketches below.
Remove the skin from the chicken leg. What do you observe?	
What happens when you flex the leg?	
Cut the tendons and examine the muscles. What do you observe?	
Cut between the thigh and drumstick to expose the joint. What do you observe?	

Logsheet 7

Plant Structure

Write a description of each plant's roots, stems, and leaves.	Make a quick sketch of each plant below. Label the parts.
Plant 1	
Plant 2	
Plant 3	

 LESSON 9

name _____

Flower Structure

Flower: _____

Write a brief description of each floral part below.	Make quick sketches below.
Sepal	
Petal	
Stamen	
Pistil	

Logsheet 9

Color Mixing

List the colors that were mixed to create the colors below.	Paint a sample of each color below.
Red	
Blue	
Yellow	
Orange	
Green	
Purple	
Brown	
Black	
Gray	

 LESSON 11

name _____

The Color Wheel

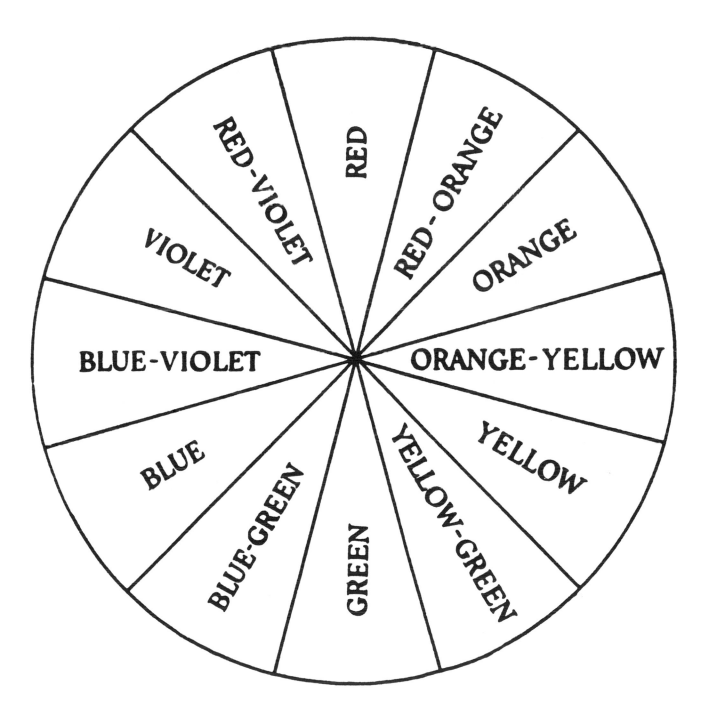

© Addison-Wesley Publishing Company

Logsheet 11

Water Interactions

Describe what happens to a water drop when it comes into contact with each substance below.	Make quick sketches below—top and side views.
Construction paper	
Newspaper	
Aluminum foil	
Wax paper	

Place several water drops on a sheet of wax paper. Describe what happens when one drop collides with another.

Logsheet 12

Who Stole the Painting?

You have just been informed that a valuable painting has been stolen from the Maintown Museum. Footprint traces indicate that the burglar removed the painting from the gallery wall, carried it through the supply room, and exited through the supply room door. Here is a map of the burglar's escape route:

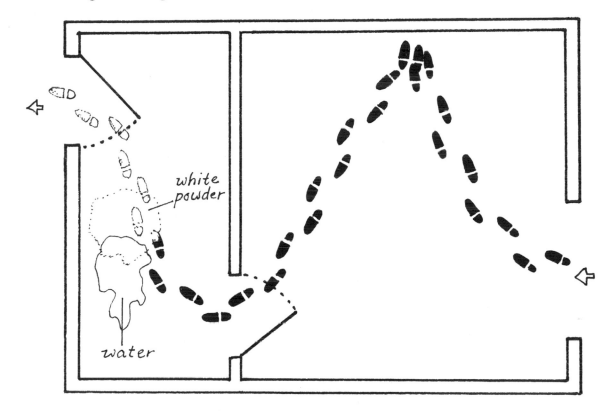

The burglar knocked over two containers on the way through the supply room. One container held a white powder, and the other held water. When you arrive at the scene of the crime, you notice that the supply room floor is covered with white powder and water. Where the two substances have mixed, a solid white material has formed.

Three suspects are being held for questioning. Each was found near the museum with white powder on his or her clothing. The first suspect is Prunella Bland, a painter. The second suspect is Emile Frost, a cook. The third suspect is Mrs. DeWitt, a board member of the art museum.

WHICH OF THESE THREE SUSPECTS STOLE THE PAINTING?

Logsheet 13

Mystery Powders

Describe each mystery substance in the areas provided.

	Observation 1 (Dry)	Observation 2 (Wet)	Observation 3 (Wet—45 minutes later)
Substance A			
Substance B			
Substance C			

Who committed the crime?   Prunella Bland–substance A
Emile Frost–substance B
Mrs. DeWitt–substance C

Identify the criminal, and explain how you came to your conclusion.
(Use back of sheet.)

Logsheet 14

Capillary Action

1. Use a hand lens to examine each paper. Describe each paper below.

Construction paper	Newspaper
Tissue paper	Facial tissue

2. Measure the height of the water in each paper. Graph the results.

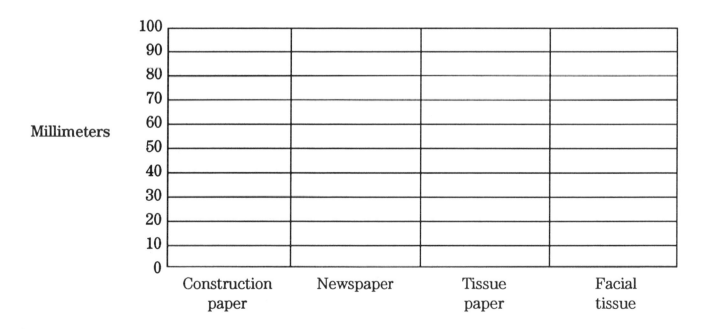

3. What general conclusion can you make, based on your results?
   (Use back of sheet.)

Logsheet 15

Paper Chromatography

Tape each test strip below.

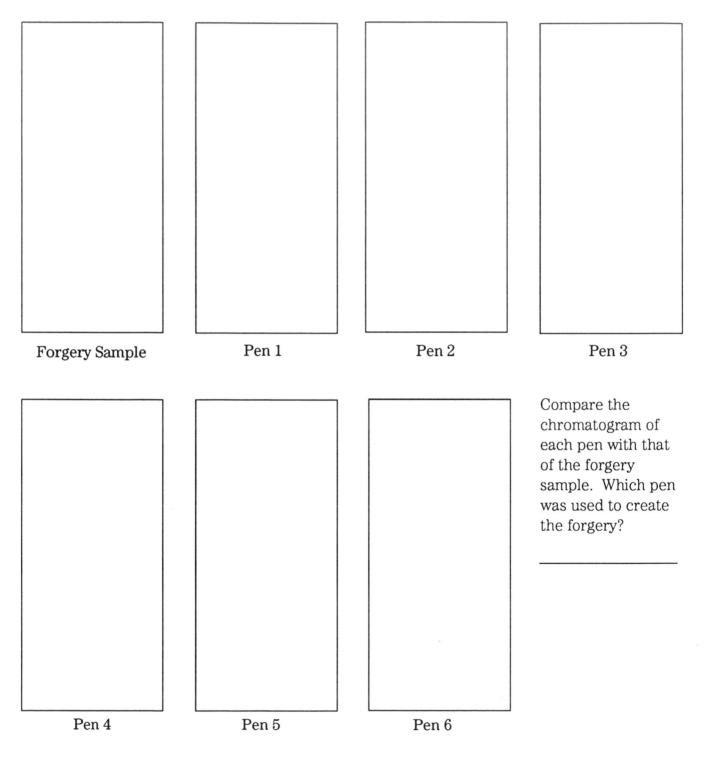

Forgery Sample   Pen 1   Pen 2   Pen 3

Pen 4   Pen 5   Pen 6

Compare the chromatogram of each pen with that of the forgery sample. Which pen was used to create the forgery?

_____

LESSON 15

Crystals

Write a description below.	Make quick sketches below larger than life-size.
Epsom salts	
Epsom salts in watercolor	

Logsheet 17

Constructing Crystalline Shapes

Cut out the patterns, and glue the tabs together.

cubic

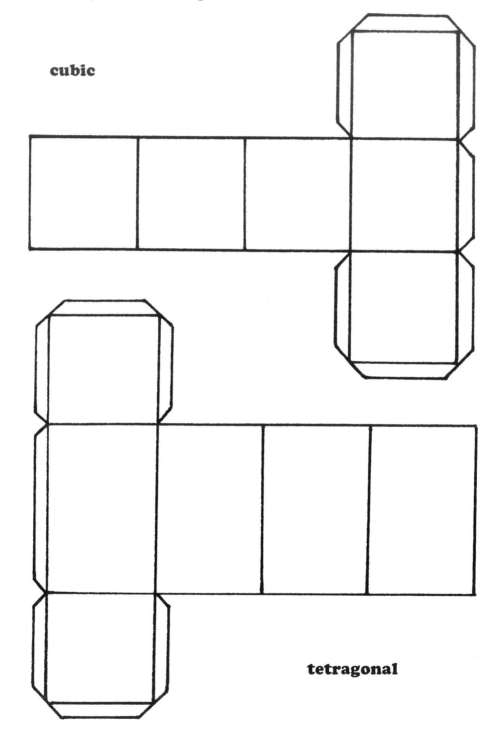

tetragonal

 LESSON 16

name _____

Constructing More Crystalline Shapes

Cut out the patterns, and glue the tabs together.

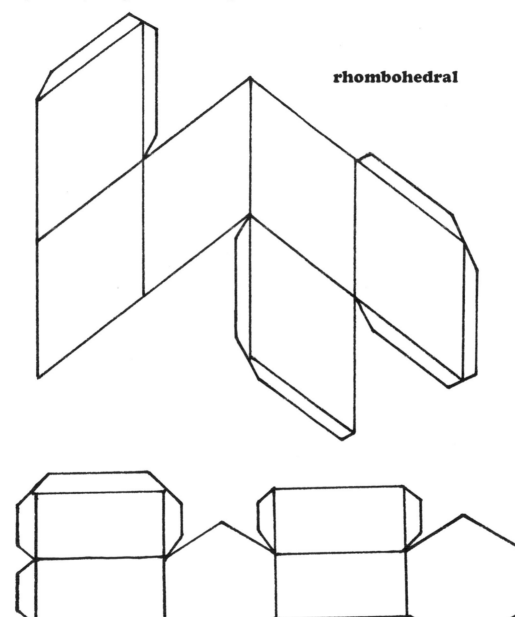

rhombohedral

hexagonal

© Addison-Wesley Publishing Company

names

Logsheet 19

Inventing a Better Chalk

Record the recipe of each chalk sample. Evaluate each sample according to its *strength*, *softness*, and *intensity*.	Attach sample chalk sketches in the spaces below.
Control sample recipe: Evaluation:	
Sample 2 recipe: Evaluation:	
Sample 3 recipe: Evaluation:	
Sample 4 recipe: Evaluation:	
Sample 5 recipe: Evaluation:	

Logsheet 20

Acids and Bases

Answer the questions below.

1. What happens when you draw a line of wet soap on the goldenrod paper?

2. What happens when you draw a line of lemon juice or vinegar on the paper?

3. What happens when you apply soap on top of the lemon juice or vinegar?

4. What happens when you apply lemon juice or vinegar on top of the soap?

name

Acid Rain

Answer the questions below.	Make quick sketches below.
What happens when the chalk is placed in water?	
What happens when the chalk is placed in vinegar?	

Logsheet 22

Outdoor Trash

Use tally marks to record the number of each kind of trash you find.

Paper	Plastic	Metal	Glass	Food	Other

Graph the totals below:

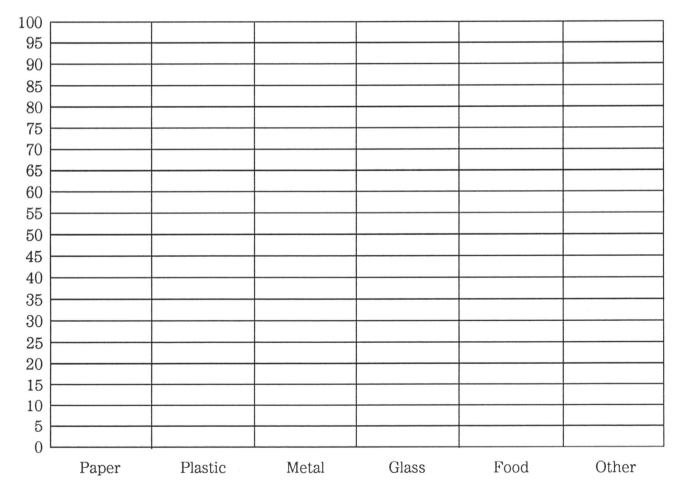

Logsheet 23

Animal Adaptations

1. Describe how each animal is adapted for *seeing, sensing, eating, hiding,* and *defending* itself.

Animal 1

Animal 2

2. List similarities and differences in the adaptations of the two animals.

Similarities	Differences
_____	_____
_____	_____
_____	_____
_____	_____
_____	_____
_____	_____

LESSON 21

Logsheet 24

Seed Classification

Place your seeds in the appropriate categories below.
Use tape to secure them to the paper.

Seeds That Float Through Air	Seeds That Fall	Seeds That Stick

Count the seeds in each category. Graph the totals below.

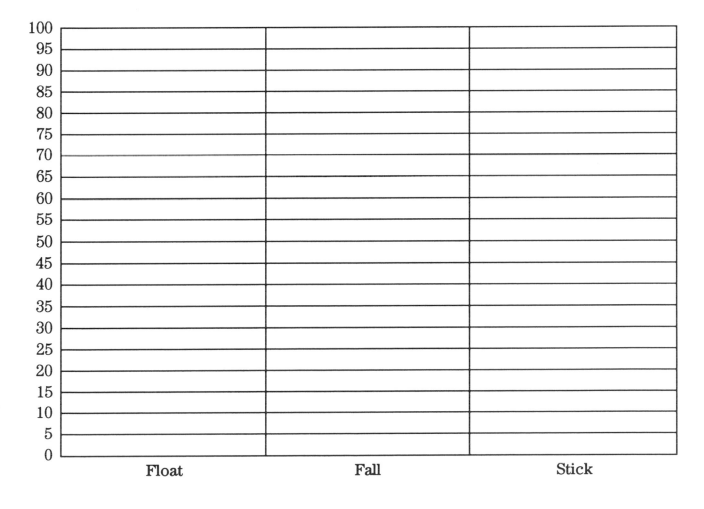

name _____

Mystery Splatters

Below each splatter, write the height from which it fell.

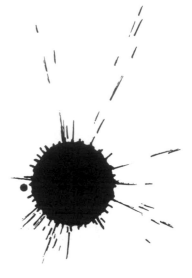

a. _____

b. _____

c. _____

d. _____

e. _____

f. _____

 LESSON 25

name _____

How Many Puffs?

Count the number of puffs required to blow each object a distance of 1 meter. Repeat the experiment for each object four times. Record the numbers, and calculate the average below.

cotton ball   1. _____   2. _____

3. _____   4. _____

Average _____

bean   1. _____   2. _____

3. _____   4. _____

Average _____

pebble   1. _____   2. _____

3. _____   4. _____

Average _____

Logsheet 27

Refraction

Carefully observe a pencil standing in a cup of water. Draw four different views below.

LESSON 28

Logsheet 28

Persistent Vision

Use crayons to sketch the afterimages produced by each figure below.

black cross	red cross
yellow cross	**blue cross**
green cross	**orange cross**

name _____

Heat Experiments

1. Calculate the net temperature change for each color house below.

black house: Starting   Final
                   temperature _____   temperature _____   Net change _____

blue house: Starting   Final
                   temperature _____   temperature _____   Net change _____

yellow house: Starting   Final
                   temperature _____   temperature _____   Net change _____

white house: Starting   Final
                   temperature _____   temperature _____   Net change _____

What are your conclusions? _____

_____

2. Calculate the net temperature change for each insulated house below.

cloth   Starting   Final
covered: temperature _____   temperature _____   Net change _____

cotton   Starting   Final
covered: temperature _____   temperature _____   Net change _____

polystyrene   Starting   Final
covered: temperature _____   temperature _____   Net change _____

cardboard   Starting   Final
covered: temperature _____   temperature _____   Net change _____

What are your conclusions? _____

_____

     LESSON 30

Appendix

Creativity Without Chaos: Management Tips

Many teachers are concerned about the management of materials and supplies during art and science lessons. Occasionally, such concerns actually prevent teachers from devoting as much time to art and science as they would like.

The key to successful, smoothly flowing lessons is good organization. With planning and preparation, you easily can manage materials and orchestrate efficient cleanup after every art and science lesson.

The following tips come from teachers who have used *The Art and Science Connection* lessons successfully in their classrooms.

How to Stay Organized

- Be sure to read each lesson all the way through before you begin.

- Give yourself time to collect all the materials you need before beginning a lesson. Many items can be brought in by students.

- Have students write their names on the back of their work at the beginning of each lesson.

- Organize students into small groups, and appoint monitors to distribute supplies before the lesson starts. Only the monitors should be allowed to leave their desks during the lesson.

Effective Cleanup Procedures

- Before beginning any lesson, make sure that students understand cleanup procedures and know where to put finished work.

- Cover desks and tables with newspaper. Students can fold odds and ends into the newspaper at cleanup time.

- Collect brushes, pencils, or other implements as a first step in cleaning up. (This stops the art activity.) One monitor can wash brushes later and stand them on their handles in a can to dry.

- Use large brown paper bags from the grocery store as trash cans for each group of students. During cleanup time, monitors can empty the bags into the regular classroom trash can, fold the bags flat, and set them aside for the next art lesson.

- Avoid sink congestion with this handy alternative: provide each student with one wet paper towel and one dry paper towel . These can be distributed loose or in a shallow tub. Have students wipe their hands with the wet towels and dry them with the dry towels, thus avoiding the sink altogether.

Tips for Working with Art Materials

Working with Tempera

- When mixing powdered tempera, add several drops of dishwashing soap to the paint. This will cause the powdered paint to dissolve more quickly in the water. A few drops of dishwashing soap in liquid tempera will cause the paint to wash off hands more easily.

- Arrange tempera paints in low containers such as cut-off milk cartons or margarine tubs with plastic lids. Arrange containers in shoe boxes for easy storage.

- Collect a variety of plastic containers to use for water. Containers of different sizes can be stored inside each other.

- Individual palettes for color mixing can be made of coffee can or margarine lids, plastic foam trays, and so on.

- When mixing colors, show students how to rinse their brushes and dry them on paper towels so as not to muddy the paints.

Working with Clay

- Use one 25-lb sack of moist clay per class. Check the clay before the lesson to be sure it is still moist.

- Use individual oilcloth place mats to cover desks. If oilcloth is not available, have students use masking tape to fasten fabric-backed wallpaper samples, heavy-duty aluminum sheets, or large flattened paper bags to their work surfaces.

- Use a length of wire for cutting the clay.

- Use plastic bags and rubber bands to store unused clay.

- Provide each group of students with a tub or bucket to wash their hands, and a dry paper towel for each student.

Working with Paste

- Distribute paste on a small scrap of paper for each student.

- When demonstrating collage, show students how to spread the paste on the back of the smaller piece of paper and then stick it to the larger piece.

- Provide wet and dry paper towels for cleanup.

Working with Watercolors

- Demonstrate how to rinse the brush thoroughly with water when mixing colors, so as to avoid muddying colors.

- Show students how to lightly dip the end of a facial tissue onto a wet watercolor pan to remove any muddy color.

- When using crayon-resist techniques, note that some colors resist wax better than others. Different colors are made with different pigments. For instance, browns are heavier than other pigments and tend to lie on the crayon rather than resist it.

- Old, dried-out watercolor pans should be discarded. After several years, the binding agent in the pigments deteriorates, and colors lose their luster.

Working with Chalk

- Reduce the amount of chalk dust produced when students use chalk. Before the activity, soak chalk pieces in water for one or two minutes, and then lay them on newspaper to dry. Using wet chalk will result in brighter colors and less dust, both in the air and on clothing.

- Another way to reduce chalk dust is to have students dip their chalk into liquid starch before applying the chalk to paper. The starch will spread the chalk color over the paper without raising dust. The same technique can be used with white liquid tempera paint on a colored construction paper background.

Tips for Working with Science Materials

The investigations in *The Art and Science Connection* make use of easily available supplies. It is often possible to substitute inexpensive materials for much of the science equipment required in standard experiments.

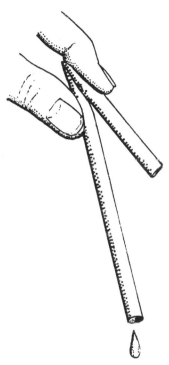

Droppers

- Use a drinking straw as a homemade dropper:

  1. Fold over the top third of the straw, and pinch the double portion of the straw (not the fold).

  2. Squeeze the straw as you dip it into the water.

  3. Stop squeezing, then lift the straw out of the water.

  4. Squeeze a little bit at a time to make drops come out.

Jars and Other Containers

- For storage, use jam, pickle, peanut butter, and baby food jars, and other types of jars that have tight-fitting lids.

- Use plastic cups of varying sizes to hold liquids during experiments. These can be rinsed thoroughly and used again.

- Use shoe boxes to organize science materials.

Trays

- A plastic foam tray makes an excellent surface on which to examine a snail or collection of pebbles.

- Aluminum pie tins are useful as waterproof trays when students are examining liquids or damp specimens.

Safety Precautions

The lessons in *The Art and Science Connection* generally make use of safe, nontoxic materials. Where more hazardous materials and procedures are called for, safety precautions are carefully outlined within the lesson.

Note: At the beginning of the school year, check with parents or guardians to determine whether any students have asthma or are allergic to any substances that might be used in a lesson.

The following points apply particularly to the activities contained in the book and are worth noting.

Art Materials: Safety Tips

- Use white glue or paste instead of resin-based glues and rubber cement.

- Use acrylic paints rather than enamel or oil paints.

- Use water-based printing inks rather than oil- or solvent-based inks.

- Use water-based felt markers rather than solvent-based markers.

- Have students wash their hands thoroughly with soap and water after art activities.

Science Materials: Safety Tips

- In handling flowers, take care that pollen is not excessively distributed through the classroom. Some students may be allergic to pollen.

- Only adults should use hot plates or irons during experiments requiring heat, while students observe.

- Caution students against placing any substance or piece of equipment in their mouths.

- Have students wash their hands thoroughly with soap and water after touching animals.

Additional Resources

The Visual Arts

Alexander, Kay. *Learning to Look and Create: The Spectra Program.* Palo Alto, Calif.: Dale Seymour, 1987.

Clements, Claire R., and Robert D. Clements. *Art and Mainstreaming: Art Instruction for Exceptional Children in Regular School Classes.* Springfield, Ill.: Charles Thomas, 1984.

Cohen, Elaine P., and Ruth S. Gainer. Art: *Another Language for Learning.* New York: Schocken Books, 1984.

Edwards, Betty. *Drawing on the Right Side of the Brain.* Los Angeles, Calif.: J.P. Tarcher, 1979.

Edwards, Betty. *Drawing on the Artist Within.* New York: Simon & Schuster, 1986.

Herberholz, Donald, and Kay Alexander. *Developing Artistic and Perceptual Awareness.* (Fifth edition). Dubuque, Ind.: William C. Brown, 1985.

Keightley, Moy. *Investigating Art: A Practical Guide for Young People.* Chicago: Facts on File, n.d.

Qualley, Charles. *Safety in the Artroom.* Worcester, Mass.: Davis Publications, 1986.

Rodgriguez, Susan. *The Special Artist's Handbook.* Palo Alto, Calif.: Dale Seymour, 1984.

Uhlin, Donald H., and Edith De Chaira. *Art for Exceptional Children.* (Third edition). Dubuque, Iowa: William C. Brown, 1984.

Wachowiak, Frank. *Emphasis Art.* (Fourth edition). New York: Thomas Y. Crowell, 1984.

Wilson, Brent, et al. *Teaching Drawing from Art.* Worcester, Mass.: Davis Publications, 1987.

Science

Allison, Linda, and David Katz. *Gee Wiz! How to Mix Art and Science or the Art of Thinking Scientifically.* Boston: Little, Brown, 1983.

Burke, James. *Connections.* Boston: Little, Brown, 1980.

DeVito, Alfred. *Creative Wellsprings for Science Teaching.* West Lafayette, Ind.: Creative Ventures, Inc., 1984.

Gross, Phyllis, and Esther P. Railton. *Teaching Science in an Outdoor Environment.* Berkeley, Calif.: University of California Press, 1972.

Hassard, Jack. *Science Experiences: Cooperative Learning and the Teaching of Science.* Menlo Park, Calif.: Addison-Wesley, 1990.

Kramer, David C. *Animals in the Classroom.* Menlo Park, Calif.: Addison-Wesley, 1989.

Lingelbach, Jenepher, ed. *Hands-On Nature: Information and Activities for Exploring the Environment with Children.* Woodstock, Vt.: Vermont Institute of Natural Science, 1987.

Lowery, Lawrence F. *The Everyday Science Sourcebook.* Palo Alto, Calif.: Dale Seymour, 1985.

Mullin, Virginia L. *Chemistry Experiments for Children.* New York: Dover, 1968.

Ostlund, Karen. *Science Process Skills, Assessing Student Performance.* Palo Alto, Calif.: Dale Seymour, 1992.

Rowe, Mary Budd. *Teaching Science as Continuous Inquiry.* (Second edition). New York: McGraw-Hill, 1978.

Science for All Americans. Washington, D.C.: American Association for the Advancement of Science, 1989.

Sisson, Edith A. *Nature with Children of All Ages.* New York: Prentice-Hall, 1982.

Skolnick, Joan, Carol Langbort, and Lucille Day. *How to Encourage Girls in Math & Science.* Englewood Cliffs, N.J.: Prentice-Hall, 1982.

Stein, Sara. *The Science Book.* New York: Workman, 1979.

Strongin, Herb. *Science on a Shoestring.* Menlo Park, Calif.: Addison-Wesley, 1991.

Cooperative Learning

Cohen, Elizabeth G. *Designing Groupwork Strategies for the Heterogeneous Classroom.* New York: Teachers College Press, 1986.

Johnson, David W., and Roger T. Johnson. *Circles of Learning: Cooperation in the Classroom.* Alexandria, Va.: Association for Supervision and Curriculum Development, 1984.

Hassard, Jack. *Science Experiences: Cooperative Learning and the Teaching of Science.* Menlo Park, Calif.: Addison-Wesley, 1990.

Kagan, Spencer. *Cooperative Learning: Resources for Teachers.* Riverside, Calif.: University of California, 1985.

Slavin, Robert E. *Using Student Team Learning.* Baltimore, Md.: Center for Social Organization of Schools, 1980.

Glossary

acceleration   The rate of change of velocity for a moving body. The acceleration may be a change in direction, a change in speed, or both.

acid   A substance that donates hydrogen ions in a chemical reaction.

adaptation   The modification of an organism or its parts that fits it better for the conditions of its environment.

adhesion   The molecular attraction between molecules of different kinds.

anatomy   The study of the internal and external structure of an organism.

anemometer   An instrument used to measure the speed of wind.

angle of incidence   The angle at which an incoming ray of light strikes a surface.

angle of reflection   The angle at which an outgoing ray of light is reflected from a surface.

Animalia   One of the kingdoms of living things that includes organisms generally capable of spontaneous movement.

animator   An artist who draws illustrations for a movie.

atom   The smallest particle of an element that can exist either alone or in combination.

baker's clay   A dough made of flour, salt, and water that is used for modeling plaques and small sculptures.

balance   The arrangement of all parts of an artwork to create a sense of equilibrium.

base   A substance that accepts hydrogen ions in a reaction.

bas-relief   A sculpture in which the forms project only slightly from the surface.

calcium sulfate   Gypsum; chemical formula $CaSO_4 \cdot 2H_2O$.

camouflage   Protective coloration that disguises an organism to hide it from its enemies.

capillaries   The smallest blood vessels of the circulatory system.

capillarity   The rising or sinking of a liquid into a small vertical space due to strong adhesion between the materials and surface tension of the liquid; also called capillary action.

carnivore   An organism that eats animals.

chemical reaction   The rearrangement of the atoms or molecules of one or more substances resulting in the creation of one or more new substances with different properties.

chromatogram   The individual color pattern produced by a mixture during the process of chromatography.

chromatography A technique used for separating mixtures.

cohesion The molecular attraction of like molecules for each other.

collage Artwork created by gluing bits of paper, fabric, scraps, photographs, or other materials to a flat surface.

color wheel An arrangement of colors in a circle that shows the relationship among primary, secondary, and complementary colors.

complementary colors The pairs of colors that lie opposite each other on the color wheel.

conductor A material through which heat travels quickly.

contrast The use of opposites in close proximity, such as light and dark, rough and smooth, and so on.

control sample An experimental sample in which all materials and procedures are the same as in the rest of the experiment but the variable being tested is not applied. For example, the chalk made of gypsum is a control sample in Inventing a Better Chalk on page 88.

crayon-resist An art technique in which crayon is applied to paper and then is covered with paint. Because wax repels water, the paint will not cover the crayoned part.

crystal A body that is formed by the solidification of a chemical element, a compound, or a mixture and has a regularly repeating internal arrangement of its atoms and often of its external structure.

crystalline Composed of crystals.

current The part of a fluid body moving continuously in a certain direction.

diffusion The scattering of light as it is reflected from an uneven surface.

emulsion A liquid dispersed throughout an immiscible liquid.

energy In science, the capacity to do work, or to make things move or grow. In the visual arts, energy is vitality of expression.

epidermis The skin, or thin surface layer of primary tissue in higher plants.

Epsom salts See magnesium sulfate.

evaporation The process by which a substance changes from a liquid to a gas.

food chain A simple model of the sequence of plant-herbivore-carnivore feeding; the passage of food and energy in an ecosystem from the primary producers through all the various consumers.

force A push or a pull.

forensic chemistry The use of chemistry to solve legal problems.

Fungi One of the kingdoms of living things that includes plantlike organisms that lack chlorophyll.

gesture drawing A drawing composed of quickly drawn lines used to indicate motion.

gravity The gravitational attraction of the earth's mass for bodies at or near its surface.

greenhouse effect A phenomenon in which infrared light rays pass through a substance, are trapped, and accumulate as heat.

gypsum See calcium sulfate.

heat Thermal energy; the random energy of motion of the molecules of matter.

herbivore An organism that eats plants.

hue Gradations of color, such as from yellow-orange to orange.

incinerator A garbage-burning plant that burns wastes under controlled high temperatures and oxygen levels, resulting in the complete combustion of the wastes.

indicator A substance that visibly shows a chemical reaction. pH paper is an acid-base indicator that changes color when a change occurs in the pH of a solution.

infrared rays Rays of light with wavelengths longer than the waves of the visible spectrum.

insulation Material through which heat travels slowly.

intensity The brightness or dullness of a color.

interaction A mutual or reciprocal action or influence.

ion An atom having either more or fewer than its normal number of electrons. An atom that has gained electrons is negatively charged and is called a negative ion. One that has lost electrons is positively charged and is called a positive ion.

joint The point of connection between bones.

landfill A large hole in the ground that is filled with garbage and then covered with soil.

law of conservation of matter A law of physics that states that matter cannot be created or destroyed; only its form can be changed.

ligament Tough band of tissue that connects bones together or holds internal organs in place.

liquid A substance that flows; the fluid state of matter in which the molecules or atoms are in contact but in which the bonding forces are too weak to hold them still with respect to one another.

magnesium sulfate Epsom salts; chemical formula $MgSO_4 \cdot 7H_2O$

magnetic force A repulsive or attractive force between the poles of magnets.

mass The quantity of matter in a body.

matter Anything that has mass and takes up space. The substance of which a physical object is composed.

membrane A thin, soft, flexible layer or skin of an organism, its structures, and/or its cells.

mirage An image of light that has been misplaced by refraction.

mixed-media The use of several different materials or techniques in one work of art.

mixture Matter containing two or more substances that are not chemically combined.

mobile A suspended sculpture with parts that can be set in motion by air currents.

molecule The smallest particle of a compound that retains the chemical identity of the compound.

Monera The kingdom that contains the simplest of living things, including bacteria, blue-green algae, and viruses.

monoprint A one-of-a-kind impression of a design or picture created on another surface.

mosaic A pattern or design made by placing many small pieces of rock, tile, glass, or other items together.

mural A work of art that is applied to a wall surface.

muscle Tissues that produce movement in the body.

negative shape A shape in an artwork that is not taken up by the subject matter but is used by the artist as part of the design.

neutralization A balance of acid and base so that hydrogen and hydroxyl ions are present in equal amounts. Neutralization produces water and a salt.

opaque Neither reflecting nor emitting light; not translucent or transparent.

pattern A regular arrangement of repeated shapes, lines, or colors.

persistent vision The holding action of the retina, which enables us to see afterimages, pictures that register in the brain for a fraction of a second after we have ceased looking at them.

pH A way of describing the acidic or basic strength of a solution. The pH value of a solution is a number on a scale from 0 to 14, with a value of 0 being extremely acidic and a value of 14 being extremely basic.

Plantae One of the kingdoms of living things that includes organisms with cell walls composed of cellulose.

plaque A flat thin piece (as of metal or clay) used for decoration.

plaster of Paris A white powdery substance used for casts and molds in the form of a quick-setting paste with water.

positive shape A shape in an artwork that forms part of its subject matter.

primary colors Red, yellow, and blue; those colors that are the basis for mixing all other colors.

protective coloration Coloration that serves to camouflage an organism, thereby hiding it from its enemies.

Protista One of the kingdoms of living things that includes some unicellular algae, protozoa, and some intermediate forms.

recycle To use again. To collect and treat a waste produce for use as a raw material.

refraction The bending of light as light rays pass at an angle from one transparent substance into another, such as from air to water.

repetition An element of design in which the artist uses repeating colors, lines, shapes, or patterns.

retina A coating of light-sensitive cells inside the back of the eye.

secondary colors Orange, green, and purple; those colors that are made by mixing pairs of primary colors.

selective reflection The reflection of only certain wavelengths from a surface material.

solid A substance that keeps its shape when it is left alone; any material whose atoms are bonded in place with respect to their nearby neighbors, giving the matter shape and strength.

solution A liquid containing another substance dissolved in it.

solvent The liquid in which the substances of a solution have dissolved.

source reduction The act of reducing the amount of waste generated at the source, such as at the home or workplace.

species A category of individuals having common attributes, the ability to interbreed, and designated a common name, such as a rose.

spectrum The rainbow spread of colors that form visible light.

splatter painting A painting made by dropping quantities of paint from various heights onto paper, canvas, or some other surface.

structure In science, the arrangement of particles or parts in a substance or body. In the visual arts, a design or organization of independent parts to form a coordinated whole.

suspension A liquid in which are mixed small undissolved particles of one or more solid substances.

symmetry An element of design in which a sense of balance is achieved by the use of identical or similar colors, lines, shapes, or designs on either side of the center.

temperature The measure of thermal energy of a substance.

tendon Tough band of white tissue that connects muscle to bone.

texture The appearance and feel of a surface: rough, smooth, bumpy, and so on.

translucent Partly transparent; admitting some light.

transparent Clear; transmitting light so that objects beyond are completely visible.

ultraviolet rays Light rays with wavelengths shorter than the waves of the visible spectrum.

value The lightness or darkness of colors.

variable A difference that causes varying results in an experiment.

variation on a theme Within a work of art, a change in form, shape, detail, or appearance that makes an object different from similar objects.

warning coloration Coloration that serves to make an organism conspicuous in its environment.

waste hierarchy Term used by the United States Environmental Protection Agency to describe the process of ranking the approaches used in a program of integrated waste management. The order of priority within the hierarchy is source reduction followed by recycling, incineration, and landfill use.

water of crystallization The state in which water molecules are included in crystals.

water of hydration Water of crystallization.

Table of Visual-Arts Media Skills

Media Skills	Lessons
Drawing	
▪ Pencil	8, 10, 28
▪ Charcoal	24
▪ Crayon	2, 12, 29
▪ Chalk	2, 13, 17
▪ Ink Pens	15, 24, 27, 29
Painting	
▪ Tempera	3, 13, 25
▪ Watercolor	11, 12, 16
▪ Food Color	4
Sculpture	
▪ Ceramic Clay	5
▪ Modeling Clay	6
▪ Chalk	19
▪ Papier Mâché	21
▪ Constructions in Space	22, 26, 30
▪ Bas-Relief	20
Collage	
▪ Mixed Media	9
▪ Murals	23
Printmaking	
▪ Gyotaku	7
Textiles	
▪ Paper Dyeing	14
Mixed Media	2, 12, 13, 18, 22

Table of Science Topics